Nigel Bishop is head teacher at Keelby Primary School in Lincolnshire. His teaching career spans 17 years. During this time, he has taught children from 4 to 11 years in a wide range of schools in Grimsby and Cleethorpes, trying to share with them his passion for experiential learning. Nigel is also a Methodist Lay Preacher and has used his communication skills in all-age worship as well as numerous school assemblies. He hopes that the stories he has used in schools and churches might reach and inspire a wider audience through their publication. Nigel lives in Grimsby with his wife, Jackie, their teenagers, Nikki and Jon, and Megan the dog. His early working years were spent on dairy, beef and arable farms in Derbyshire and Lincolnshire, followed by a period of pastoral and youth work for the Methodist Church in Derby. It was here that he felt drawn to a classroom vocation and converted his BSc degree in Agriculture into a PGCE teaching qualification and, subsequently, an MEd.

7

D1148645

WORCESTERSHIRE COUNTY COUNCIL	
303	
Bertrams	07.10.06
379.28	£6.99
WS	

Text copyright © Nigel Bishop 2006
The author asserts the moral right
to be identified as the author of this work

Published by
The Bible Reading Fellowship
First Floor, Elsfield Hall
15–17 Elsfield Way, Oxford OX2 8FG
Website: www.brf.org.uk

ISBN-10: 1 84101 465 6
ISBN-13: 978 1 84101 465 4

First published 2006
10 9 8 7 6 5 4 3 2 1 0
All rights reserved

Acknowledgments
Scripture quotations are taken from the Contemporary English Version of the Bible published
by HarperCollins Publishers, copyright © 1991, 1992, 1995 American Bible Society.

A catalogue record for this book is available from the British Library

Printed in Singapore by Craft Print International Ltd

Stories

FOR INTERACTIVE ASSEMBLIES

15 story-based assemblies to get children talking

NIGEL BISHOP

Dedicated to Mum and Dad, whose love for each other
and for others is a constant inspiration

ACKNOWLEDGMENT

With thanks to countless colleagues and friends,
to Nikki, Jon and Dave for proofreading the original stories,
to Sue at BRF for her encouragement and support,
and to Jackie who continues to believe in me in spite of everything.

CURRICULUM LINKS: NOTE TO TEACHERS

Curriculum references refer to non-statutory guidelines for PSHE and Citizenship at Key Stage 2 and the non-statutory national framework for RE. References are correct at the time of going to press. Non-statutory guidelines for PSHE and Citizenship can be accessed through the Teachernet website, www.teachernet.gov.uk. The non-statutory national framework for RE can be accessed through the Qualifications and Curriculum Authority website, www.qca.org.uk. Should any changes be made to the detailed objectives at some time in the future, please refer to the respective websites for information.

Contents

Foreword

Using the storytelling style of Jesus, Nigel Bishop has created stories firmly rooted in the experiences of the intended audience. Instead of a farmer's field or the road to Jericho, a school classroom or hall provides the backdrop for these thought-provoking parables. The immediate connection to the child's world will not fail to engage the listener and bring the stories to life. The stories, followed by the suggested questions, will open minds and enable pupils to explore the messages and metaphors hidden within the parables.

The stories are of infinitely more worth because no explanation of possible meaning has been given. Therefore, the children are encouraged to interpret and discover for themselves how the stories relate to their lives, values, behaviour and relationships. These thought processes will enrich and illuminate their own spiritual journeys.

These stories will appeal to children from all faiths and cultural backgrounds and could be used in primary schools throughout the country. As Nigel suggests in his introduction, telling the stories rather than reading them would make a greater impact. So I would like to encourage you to 'go for it' and perhaps dare to make slight adjustments, making the stories more relevant to your pupils.

Nigel Bishop has clearly used his wide range of teaching and preaching experiences to fulfil his intention of providing a resource that will open up the Gospel parables to new audiences while remaining true to their original author.

Lisa Fenton, Senior Adviser to Schools, Blackburn Diocese

Introduction

The stories that Jesus told to convey so much of his teaching to a variety of audiences are known as 'parables', and they were a narrative form used by many rabbis, or Jewish teachers, of his day. There has been a great deal of debate over the years about just how the parables should be interpreted. Parables can be riddles, illustrative stories, proverbs, allegories, extended metaphors and similitudes (for example, 'The kingdom of heaven is like this…').

Parables have been described as 'earthly stories with a heavenly meaning', but it is clear that Jesus used them to communicate what he considered to be great truths about his vision for a new society as well as his ideas on spirituality. They share the good news, or 'gospel', of God's inclusive love and sovereign generosity; they describe the nature of the kingdom of God, how it comes and how it grows; they define the qualities looked for in the people of this new society, and they allude to the purpose of Jesus' own life and death.

As a means of teaching, the parables have a number of characteristics going for them. These stories, set in contexts easily accessible to those who hear them, are vivid, challenging and memorable. Jesus taught a variety of audiences, divided loosely into three groups: his disciples (or chosen close friends), his enemies (usually the ultra-religious people of his day, the scribes and Pharisees) and the crowds of ordinary people who flocked to hear him preach. It was for this last group that the parables were most often employed, according to the Gospel narratives. The attraction of the parabolic form lies in the apparent clarity of the story (although at times this includes an inherent strangeness or unexpected twist), coupled with a tendency to provoke further reflection and appropriate action in the listener. As C.H. Dodd put it, a parable 'leaves the mind in sufficient doubt about its application to tease it into active thought'. In similar vein, P.G. Wodehouse explained that a parable 'kept something up its sleeve' which was capable of striking its hearer later.

From the time of the early Church through to the 19th century, the parables of Jesus were treated by most scholars as complete allegories. Detailed and dogmatic spiritual interpretations were attached to every aspect of a story, leaving almost no room for interpretation by the listener or reader. Presumably if you weren't 'in the know' about these conventions you were missing out on the 'truths' shared by the initiated. In this way, an originally inclusive and creative piece of storytelling became exclusive and narrow. It is generally felt that the parables are the most accurately recorded aspects of Jesus' teaching, apart from some interpretation that appears to have been added. The only real claim that they might have been stories containing truths intended only for the chosen few comes in Mark 4:10–12 (reworked in Matthew and Luke), although this may well be a personal theory of the Gospel writer. Certainly the nature of the parables and the way in which they were told suggest an attempt by Jesus to reach as wide an audience as possible with his groundbreaking teaching.

Consequently, the modern trend has been to view the parables less as allegories and more as illustrative stories containing a limited number of parallels with spiritual or societal truths. For example, a parable like 'The prodigal son' speaks of the forgiving love of God, but also has a great deal to say about the nature of jealousy, as exemplified by the older brother's reaction to what might otherwise have been good news. During the 20th century, biblical scholars have opened up our interpretation of the parables, and in the postmodern age we are increasingly likely to view these stories as instruments through which their original author can reach directly into the minds of those who hear them, providing almost as many responses as there are people to respond. Jesus' vision of reality gave rise to the parable narratives, the purpose of which was to produce in his listeners an effect that changed how they thought about the world and lived their lives in it.

As a Methodist preacher and primary school teacher, I have become increasingly convinced that the very essence of these powerful and authentic stories of Jesus is being lost to generations of listeners. This is partly due to our tendency to read rather than tell them in acts of worship or assemblies. More significantly, however, I believe that the obscure contexts in which the parables are set makes them almost impossible for many listeners to engage with. I vividly remember from my childhood a dramatized version of the good Samaritan set in a railway carriage. Suddenly the story came alive for me, because I could relate to the characters and events as being real rather than biblical. This was a story about life as I knew it, rather than life in some distant time and country. It was connected to my own experiences, my own hopes and fears, rather than being the stuff of slides of the Holy Land and Sunday school photocopies.

For several years now, I have reworked the parables of Jesus for all-age worship in local Methodist churches and the schools in which I have led assemblies. My intention in this book is to record for you some of the stories I have used. I almost always *tell* the stories (rather than reading them), adapting the names and some of the events to suit the context in which I find myself. I have 'road tested' these written accounts with a variety of audiences, and I trust you will feel that they get the point across if you choose to read them out loud. However, I do urge you to throw caution to the winds and *tell* them wherever you can. The details, after all, are not so very important—it's the central, lifestyle-challenging idea that's vital.

When I have finished reading or telling one of these stories, I invariably ask, 'Who told this story first?' When someone replies 'Jesus', I explain that I have changed the setting, but that I hope the meaning has stayed the same. It's amazing how rapidly heads start bobbing, fingers fiddling and eyes wandering as soon as any attempt at interpretation starts. Following the example of Jesus, the master storyteller, I have found that it is far better just to let the parable speak for itself. I suggest, therefore, that the follow-up work included in this book would be best used at a later time, perhaps in another place, although I am currently experimenting with short periods of paired talk in my services and assemblies, to enable immediate responses from the listeners.

Some of the stories are not immediately or easily recognizable to those who know the originals. I have located them all either in a primary school setting or one readily recognizable to children of 4–11 years of age. They are intended to be contemporary, although such is the pace of change in education (and society in general) that I am sure they will soon appear dated and you may need to adjust them to keep them fresh for your audience. I have used them in a multi-faith context as part of acts of worship of a 'broadly Christian' nature at school. At the end of each story I have given a biblical text explaining where my inspiration came from, although it is not my intention that readers or listeners would go straight to their Bibles in order to look up the original. This would defeat the purpose of using a contemporary setting to challenge children in a new way. I recommend that the preparation and follow-up activities are completed without reference to the Bible, although of course I would encourage children to look up the texts in an appropriate translation later if they are interested. My main intention, of course, has been to provide a resource which will open up the parables to a new audience, while remaining faithful to the vision of their originator, whose words have proved life-changing to so many for so long.

THE PARABLES

The titles of the original parables, as shown below, are taken from the Contemporary English Version of the Bible (CEV).

1. A story about three servants: Matthew 25:14–30
2. The good Samaritan: Luke 10:25–37
3. The two builders: Luke 6:46–49
4. The great banquet: Luke 14:15–24

5.   Weeds among the wheat: Matthew 13:24–30
6.   A story about ten girls: Matthew 25:1–13
7.   One sheep: Luke 15:4–7
8.   An official who refused to forgive: Matthew 18:21–35
9.   Two sons: Luke 15:11–32
10. A story about a farmer: Matthew 13:3–8
11. A Pharisee and a tax collector: Luke 18:9–14
12. A valuable pearl: Matthew 13:45–46
13. A story about two sons: Matthew 21:28–31
14. A hidden treasure: Matthew 13:44
15. Workers in a vineyard: Matthew 20:1–16

The three monitors

TARGET

Making the most of talents and abilities

Mr Gallant had to go on a computer course, so he asked for three monitors to meet him in his classroom during lunch time, and left each one a job to do for the supply teacher the following day.

Jonathan was a good reader and meticulously neat, so Mr Gallant asked him to tidy the bookshelf just before home time.

'Make sure the library books are separate from the reading scheme ones,' explained Mr Gallant carefully. 'Oh, and please make sure all the spines are facing outwards as well, so that people can see the titles,' he added as an afterthought.

Kirsty loved plants and animals—well, anything to do with nature really—so Mr Gallant showed her where the watering can was and took her to each of the plants, telling her how much water they would need.

Matthew, the least reliable of the three monitors, gazed up into Mr Gallant's face, noticing the thoughtful expression.

'What on earth can I give him to do?' wondered the teacher, racking his brains for something useful but not difficult, or delicate, or dangerous. Then it occurred to him. Of course…

'Matthew,' he said encouragingly, 'you can wipe the whiteboard for me.'

Matthew's face showed no real sign of confidence as he cautiously nodded, but Mr Gallant decided that there was very little that could possibly go wrong. In fact, he went home that night with a light heart, looking forward to his computer course the next day, and anticipating a pleasant return to school the day after.

Mr Gallant whistled cheerfully to himself as he sauntered across the playground two days later. The car had started first time, he had cheese and pickle sandwiches in his lunchbox and he was looking forward to trying out some of the computer skills he'd learnt on his course—if he could get the machine started, that was.

Jonathan left the football match, which was already in full swing even at ten to nine, and intercepted his teacher just as Mr Gallant's hand was reaching out to open the door into school.

'I did the books,' proclaimed Jonathan with pride. 'I put the spines out, like you said, and I put them in alphabetical order—by author—like they told us that time on our library visit,' he added by way of explanation.

'Well done, Jonathan, you're a complete star,' said Mr Gallant, beaming broadly. 'I knew you'd make a good job, but I didn't imagine you'd do all that. You can be the class librarian every week if you like. Come inside and I'll find you a treat.'

The two of them were about to go inside when Kirsty ran up, her rucksack banging noisily against her back.

'I watered the plants—like you said,' she panted breathlessly. 'I wiped the dust off all the leaves too. And I took the dead leaves out of the pots for you.'

'That's marvellous, Kirsty,' said Mr Gallant approvingly. 'I knew you'd be OK, although I thought the watering would be hard enough. You can be the class gardener from now on. Come inside and I'll find you a treat.'

As they passed through the doorway, Mr Gallant suddenly remembered Matthew. He turned and walked back down the steps on to the playground, searching the mass of bobbing heads for the last monitor. He spotted him in a corner of the playground, hands in pockets, head down, shoulders hunched. Mr Gallant got the distinct impression that Matthew was avoiding him, so he called his name and beckoned him over with a few rapid movements of his finger.

'How did you get on yesterday?' he enquired when the boy eventually reached him.

'Fine,' came the reply.

'Did Mrs Gaynor have any problems with anything? Or anyone?' asked Mr Gallant pointedly.

'No,' replied Matthew with wide, honest eyes.

'Did you do the board for me?'

No answer—not at first. And then, after careful consideration, Matthew explained sulkily.

'I knew it wouldn't be good enough for you. I thought I might smudge the board, or rub off something I shouldn't, and I didn't want to get into trouble, so... I left it.'

Matthew looked up uncertainly, waiting to see what would happen.

'Oh, Matthew,' said Mr Gallant. 'You could at least have had a go. You can stay out here on the playground until the bell goes and think about it. I was going to take you in for a treat, but I'll split it between the other two. They took the opportunities I gave them and did extra work as well.'

But looking at the dispirited boy before him, and thinking for a moment about all the things that might have gone wrong yesterday, Mr Gallant felt he should say a bit more.

'If you don't try to do things, you'll never get anywhere in life. Next time I give you a job, give it a try. I'll be much happier if you do, and so will you, even if it doesn't quite work out.'

I wonder if there was a next time. What do you think?

(Find this story as Jesus told it in Matthew 25:14–30.)

CURRICULUM LINKS

PSHE KS1: 1b share opinions; 1e set goals; 2c recognize choices; 2e responsibilities; 2h contribute to life; 4b work co-operatively; 5a take responsibility; 5b feel positive; 5c discussions.

PSHE KS2: 1a talk and write about opinions; 1b recognize their worth, set personal goals; 1e develop skills; 2d responsibilities and duties; 5a take responsibility; 5b feel positive about themselves; 5f develop relationships.

RE KS1: 1a explore religious stories; 1d religious beliefs in the arts; 2c identify what matters to them and others; 2d reflect on moral values and their own behaviour; 3j belonging; 3k myself; 3p sharing their own beliefs, ideas and values.

RE KS2: 1a describe stories; 1f religious responses to ethical questions; 2c discuss religious belief; 3o discussing religious and philosophical questions; 3p considering experiences and feelings.

MENTAL SWITCH-ON

How do you feel about doing jobs for teachers? Why do they ask children to do jobs for them? What kinds of children normally get asked to do jobs? Do you need to receive a reward for doing a job around school?

SO WHAT?

- How do you think each of the children in the story felt about being asked to do something by Mr Gallant?
- What could Matthew have done to get help with his fears about wiping the board properly?

- Can you remember a time when you didn't do something because you were afraid you couldn't do it well enough?
- What do you think you're good at?
- What talents or abilities would you like to use more?
- When might it be OK to make mistakes at school?
- How important is it for people to use the talents they have?
- Which talents are the most useful to other people?
- What does the story say about the way Jesus thought people should behave?

PRAYER

Help us to know what we can do,
help us to practise until we improve,
and help us to believe we can achieve great things
for others, for ourselves and for you. Amen

POSSIBILITIES

Visual ideas

Suggest that the children draw pictures or write a list of jobs they've done at school and at home. Next to this, they could add the jobs that they'd like to do. As an extension, the more able could try to identify particular skills or knowledge that they have used in each job. Their identified skills and knowledge could each be accompanied by an icon to help children remember them, and then be displayed on cards to share with the class.

Auditory ideas

Ask groups of children to act out the last scene of the story, when Mr Gallant walked through the playground.

An extension for the more able might be to write a dialogue between Matthew and one of the other two children during the next playtime. The children could work out an acrostic based on the word TALENTS to share out loud with the rest of the class.

Kinaesthetic ideas

Each child writes his or her name on a piece of paper and leaves it on the table where they sit. Everyone then circulates round the room, adding to the sheets the skills and talents that they think other children possess, until every child's paper has at least three. At this point the teacher could gather the children into a circle and ask each child to share what has been written about them. A variation would be for children to read out someone else's list.

Younger or less able children could be given three cards, each preprinted by the teacher with a different skill or talent: for example, helpful, kind, tidy, busy, friendly, funny and so on. The children can then circulate round the room, placing each card under another child's name.

Tactile ideas

Ask the children to make a dice using a cube net. They could then write on each face a talent based on a character trait, perhaps read from the board following a class or group discussion. In groups, they could then roll the dice and take it in turns to think of something they have done recently, or could do in the future, which is an example of the talent shown.

Group ideas

Give each child their name on a card, and ask them to put it somewhere in the class to show a job they have done or a job they would like to do. They could discuss together what training they would need to tackle some of the harder jobs.

The whole class could sit in a circle and, while the teacher holds up each card in turn, the children could take it in turns to call out that person's talents.

Organize the children to work in groups to produce a fund-raising idea for a charity of their choice, drawing on ideas and skills within the group or class. Small groups of children could draw up a rota for class jobs and then put their names on it using sticky notes.

The class pain

TARGET

Avoiding prejudice

Pritveh was taking the register. Finally he'd been chosen. He couldn't believe it—the number of times he'd put his hand up and been overlooked by Miss Stamp. Now his moment had come and he was determined to enjoy the freedom and excitement of walking the whole length of the school.

However, it wasn't long before he started to have second thoughts. He was only in Year Three, and it seemed a shame that the teachers had all been told to send only one person to the office on any errand. He had to pass the Year Six cloakrooms, and now the stories he'd heard of all the horrible things that could happen to you there came flooding back into his mind. Pritveh stopped, took a deep breath, lowered his head and almost ran down the corridor past the coats and bags that crowded the pegs on both walls.

It was as he first detected the smell of the boys' toilets in his fear-widened nostrils that Pritveh ran smack into the very solid form of Wayne Nelson. The register and dinner money tin clattered to the floor, and as the Year Three stooped to pick them up a trainer clumped down on top of each of them. The trainers were not the same—one was white and the other red, and neither of them belonged to Wayne. As Pritveh looked up terrified from his kneeling position, he found himself surrounded by three boys, their manner intimidating and their faces uncompromising. Miss Stamp's safe, warm classroom seemed a million miles away.

'What have we got here?' sneered one of the boys. He was smaller than Pritveh, but he had a mean, nasty expression on his narrow face that spoke of imminent unpleasantness. Pritveh didn't know his name, but he'd met him before on the playground.

'You've dropped the register,' joined in his sidekick, another boy whose name Pritveh didn't know, although his ugly, fat face and matching body were instantly recognizable. 'It might get all messed up on the floor there, and then you'd get into big trouble at the office, wouldn't you?' he continued, menacingly.

'Unless, of course, you gave us your tuck money.' This suggestion came from Wayne himself, the toughest boy in the school. Even the teachers seemed to be scared of him sometimes. He switched on a grin, one full of menace but tinged with obvious enjoyment. Pritveh thrust his right hand quickly into his pocket, pulled out the 50 pence coin with trembling, moist fingers and cautiously held it out towards Wayne. Fat Face grabbed it, crushing the delicate brown fingers as he did so, while Narrow Face delivered a punch and a kick that drew tears instantly to Pritveh's eyes, as well as doubling him over in mouth-twisting pain on to the tiled floor, where he lay in a sobbing ball. Pritveh's mind was spinning with a mixture of fear, hurt and anger. He clutched his head, as if he could hug the feelings away, and wriggled into the cover of the coats on the right-hand side of the corridor.

If Pritveh had looked around at this point, he would have been surprised by the speed with which the three Year Sixes had disappeared. He would also have been very relieved. But right now he didn't look. He didn't listen. He just crouched there, sniffling and shaking miserably, his big trip completely spoiled.

Lauren was on the way to the hall when she saw him. She had been chosen to read the story in assembly today and had been told that she could go and practise for two minutes. She didn't know the boy, although she knew he was younger than her, but she told herself she hadn't time to stop and hurried past on the left-hand side of the corridor so as not to disturb him.

David was also on the way to the hall. He had the important job of setting up the digital projector and he was proud of the fact that he hadn't missed a single assembly all year. When he saw Pritveh, he had a sudden recollection of being in a similar place when he was that age. He looked swiftly and fearfully around him, realized that there was no threat, but nevertheless tiptoed carefully past the huddled, crying boy. Once past, he speeded up again, his mind set on the task ahead.

Samantha was on her way to see the school nurse. It seemed as though she was always going to see her for one thing or another. The other kids often whispered about her, their hands in front of their mouths while their eyes, full of contempt, stabbed across the room into hers. Everyone in Year Five said she was a pain. She could tell that the teachers thought it sometimes too, although they never actually said so. Everyone knew she smelled. That was why everyone avoided her when the class lined up for assembly. At least she would be spared that embarrassment today.

When she came round the corner, she saw Pritveh and felt sorry for him. She could instantly imagine what had happened. She retrieved the register and tin, put her arm around him and led him to the office where Mrs Baxter soon brought the whole story flooding out of him.

'He can have my tuck money, Miss,' offered Samantha, holding out a number of silver coins on a dirt-grimed hand. 'I'll come back after I've seen the nurse if you like. Then I can take him back to class for you.'

Not such a pain after all, then.

(Find this story as Jesus told it in Luke 10:25–37.)

CURRICULUM LINKS

PSHE KS1: 1a fair and unfair, right and wrong; 1b share opinions; 1c recognize and deal with feelings; 2a discussions; 2c recognize choices, right and wrong; 2e needs and responsibilities; 2h contribute to life; 4b work co-operatively; 4c differences and similarities; 4d friends should care; 4e bullying; 5a take responsibility; 5b feel positive; 5c discussions; 5g moral dilemmas.

PSHE KS2: 1a talk and write about opinions; 1b recognize their worth, set personal goals; 1e develop skills; 2d responsibilities and duties; 2k explore the media; 3e recognize risks; 4a care about others; 4e challenge stereotypes; 4f differences and similarities; 5a take responsibility; 5b feel positive about themselves; 5f develop relationships; 5g moral dilemmas.

RE KS1: 1a explore religious stories; 1d religious beliefs in the arts; 2c identify what matters to them and others; 2d reflect on moral values and their own behaviour; 3j belonging; 3k myself; 3p sharing their own beliefs, ideas and values.

RE KS2: 1a describe stories; 1f religious responses to ethical questions; 2c discuss religious belief; 2d right and wrong; 3f teachings and authority; 3k following a religion or belief; 3m fairness; 3o discussing religious and philosophical questions; 3p considering experiences and feelings.

MENTAL SWITCH-ON

What might make someone frightened at school? How do you keep safe when there are no adults about? What does it mean to judge someone? Who have you judged recently?

SO WHAT?

- How did Pritveh's feelings about going to the office change after the older boys had taken his tuck money?
- As they had been given important jobs by teachers, what kind of children do you think Lauren and David were?
- Why didn't they stop to help Pritveh?
- When might it be more important to go and do a job than to stop and help someone in trouble?
- How do you think Samantha felt about her classmates?
- Jesus told the original story to answer a man who asked, 'Who should I care for?' Which child in the story cared for someone?
- Why was Samantha's reaction surprising?
- Why was it important for Pritveh to tell someone what had happened?
- What do you think this story has to say about pre-judging people (or prejudice)?

PRAYER

Give us the wisdom to see the good in those around us,
give us the friendship to help those who need us,
give us the courage to stand up for those who are alone.
Amen

POSSIBILITIES

Visual ideas

Ask the children to draw a picture of the faces of the different characters in the story, showing their expressions. An extension for the more able could be to identify pairs of characters whose actions affected the feelings of others: for example, Wayne and Pritveh, Pritveh and Lauren, Samantha and Pritveh. The pupils could write alongside each pair how one affected the other.

Another activity would be to get children to draw a graph of

Pritveh's feelings throughout the story (how happy he is, from 0 to 10). An extension would be to add in other characters—for example, Wayne, Lauren and so on—to see how their emotions were affected by their encounters with Pritveh.

Auditory ideas

Provide a group of children with some percussion instruments and ask them to devise backing sounds to match part, or all, of the story. For younger or less able children, a recording of the text by the teacher could be provided for them to work to, rather than asking one of them to read aloud. A performance could be shared with the rest of the class at the end of the lesson.

Kinaesthetic ideas

On a plan of the school the children could identify areas where children might not feel safe from bullying. This could involve taking turns to tour the school in pairs, with groups getting together to discuss their results. Finally, a plan with 'hotspots' identified could be shared with the rest of the class and perhaps the school council, so that the staff could consider solutions.

Tactile ideas

The children could be given some newspapers and asked to find and cut out photographs of, or stories about, people who are judged by society and can be easily stereotyped (for example, footballers with their bad behaviour). The children could then write or copy words that contrast with our preconceptions on to a collage of the pictures.

Group ideas

Groups of children might each be given a set of cards with the following behaviours on them. They could then try to agree how to place them in order on their table, with the 'worst' at one end and the 'best' at the other:

punching
helping
stealing
kicking
name calling
encouraging
teasing
sharing
listening
provoking
giving
ignoring
laughing
befriending

Ask groups of children to produce tableaux of each key scene in the story. The rest of the class take it in turns to study each tableau and decide which person is playing each character, based on their pose and facial expression.

The class assembly

```
TARGET
Building on a strong foundation
```

'It's our class assembly next week,' announced Miss Butcher with rather strained enthusiasm. It was the summer term and everyone was getting ready for a break. She wasn't too sure about the theme she'd been given, but she knew she had to make the best of it. It was 'Concern for others', and there were only five working days to get something ready that would impress the rest of the staff, the head teacher and all the masses of parents who she knew would turn up.

The class was immediately enthusiastic, which gave Miss Butcher quite a lift and reassured her that it would be all right. A forest of hands went up when she asked for ideas for a short play about how the children could help one another, and how they could get involved in helping to change life for other people.

'We could tell them about all the fund-raising we've done in school this year,' suggested Hanadi energetically. 'Like that cake bake for wells in India and the sponsored readathon to buy books for Africa.'

'What about doing a play about disability?' said Alex, leaning forward from his wheelchair to grab his drafting book. 'I could start writing something now,' he added, seizing a pencil with obvious intent.

'Let's all spend the next 20 minutes working in twos to come up with some more concrete ideas,' Miss Butcher replied. 'Then we can share them with each other and vote for the best ones.'

Alex and Charlie's sketch about a sports day won the vote for a piece of drama. It was about some children who devised a sitting throw event because their friend couldn't take part in the obstacle course for health and safety reasons. By lunch time Miss Butcher was feeling much better.

Alex had offered to play the part of the disabled boy. As he put it himself, his wheelchair did give him a head start. He busied himself on the computer during lunch time, producing scripts for the other cast members, and that night he marked his lines using a green highlighter. His mum practised his words with him for an hour until he was sure of all of them. He couldn't wait for tomorrow's rehearsal.

By contrast, Charlie found several more pressing things to do that night. He had a quick look at his lines, decided that they could wait until the weekend, and disappeared out on to the street in search of his mates. His stepdad offered to look at the script with him but Charlie declined the offer. Besides, there was a match on the telly that he had to watch.

After registration the next afternoon, Miss Butcher took the class down to the hall for a first runthrough. A piece of dance had been worked out during morning break, based on a chart album that someone had brought in. Some facts and figures about the developing world had been researched by Hanadi and some of her friends, along with an account of what the school had done to make a difference. There was a map and a number of large pieces of paper that were going to be turned into a computer presentation by the day of the assembly next week. They all practised the two songs that were to be used, and a group of boys who'd gone off to compose a piece of percussion music returned to perform their masterpiece. It was called 'The Outcast', they said, and when you heard it you certainly knew why. Miss Butcher said it was lovely and nobody argued. Anyway, everybody had a pretty good idea that they couldn't have done any better themselves.

Finally it was time for the sketch. The performers took their positions and the action started. It soon became clear that most of the cast knew their lines. However, in the final scene where Charlie and Alex had to demonstrate the sitting throw event and discuss the result of the competition, it became equally clear that Charlie had a lot of work to do.

Alex wasn't just saying the words as they were written. He was already putting in all the meaning. Nobody had ever seen a first rehearsal like it.

Charlie's performance was in a different league—'one of the lower ones', he would have said if it had been a football match. Half the time he couldn't find his place, and when he did, he found it impossible to get his mouth round the words.

'You really need to look at those lines over the weekend, Charlie,' suggested Miss Butcher nervously.

In class at home time, he made a point of getting them out on his table and having a quick glance at them, but his mind was on the film he was going to see with his dad that night. Unfortunately the script seemed to have slipped out of his bag when he got home. 'Never mind,' he thought. 'I can always get another copy on Monday.'

There was a real buzz in the hall as the assembly began. The head teacher, Mrs Presley, introduced the class and then settled into a chair at the side with an expectant look on her cheerful face. Miss Butcher had a much more tense look about her, but as the performance began she relaxed visibly. The world was about to become a much sunnier place for her. If only they could all get through it without a hitch.

Everyone enjoyed the first song—it had great actions, which were always a hit, especially with the infants. The dance was fine. So was the computer presentation, with both the laptop and the projector behaving themselves perfectly. The world premier of 'The Outcast' was received with polite applause. Then came the sketch. Alex was as wordperfect as ever, and the feeling he managed to get into his performance had to be seen to be believed.

As for Charlie, let's just say that it wasn't his finest hour. His stepdad was seen shaking his head repeatedly, and at one point he even put his head in his hands. As Mrs Presley commented afterwards when she bumped into Charlie in the dining-room, 'If a job's worth doing, it's worth doing well.'

He'd already apologized by then to Alex and Miss Butcher. He liked to think he'd learnt his lesson this time, but I wonder.

(Find this story as Jesus told it in Luke 6:46–49.)

CURRICULUM LINKS

PSHE KS1: 1b share opinions; 1c recognize and deal with feelings; 1d think about themselves; 2a discussions; 2c recognize choices; 2d agree and follow rules; 2e needs and responsibilities; 2h contribute to life; 3a simple choices that improve well-being; 4a behaviour affects others; 4b work co-operatively; 4c differences and similarities; 5a take responsibility; 5b feel positive; 5c discussions; 5d real choices.

PSHE KS2: 1a talk and write about opinions; 1b recognize their worth, seeing mistakes, setting personal goals; 1e develop skills; 2b making and changing rules; 2d responsibilities and duties; 3a mental health; 4a care about others; 4f differences and similarities; 5a take responsibility; 5b feel positive about themselves.

RE KS1: 1a explore religious stories; 1d religious beliefs in the arts; 2c identify what matters to them and others; 2d reflect on moral values and their own behaviour; 3j belonging; 3k myself; 3p sharing their own beliefs, ideas and values.

RE KS2: 1a describe stories; 1f religious responses to ethical questions; 2c discuss religious belief; 2d right and wrong; 3f teachings and authority; 3k following a religion or belief; 3m fairness; 3o discussing religious and philosophical questions; 3p considering experiences and feelings.

MENTAL SWITCH-ON

How do you feel about doing class assemblies or Christmas shows? What's the hardest part about learning lines? How do teachers feel about doing assemblies with their classes?

SO WHAT?

- What were the members of Miss Butcher's class good at doing as they prepared for the assembly?
- How would you describe Alex and Charlie?
- What was the biggest difference between the way the two boys approached the assembly?
- What else might Miss Butcher have done with Charlie when she realized he was struggling with his lines?
- Why do you think she left him to make his own decision?
- How do you think Charlie felt when he made a mess of his performance?
- What might Alex have said to him afterwards?
- What does the story say about how Jesus would want his friends to live?
- How do you organize your life so that work is balanced with play?

PRAYER

Success is built on hard work,
like a well rehearsed assembly.
Being part of a team
means taking responsibility.
And healthy living
needs a balance between work and play.
Through the whole of our lives
please show us the way. Amen

POSSIBILITIES

Visual ideas

Ask each child to draw a mind-map of their life, showing the balance between work and play, both at home and at school. Younger or less able children could draw a picture split down the middle showing work and play.

The children could write a diary entry for Charlie, showing his recollection of the events of the day of the assembly, and describing his feelings about not being prepared. The more able children could write a resolution or motto for Charlie as he tries to do better next time.

Auditory ideas

Ask the children to work in pairs, discussing their views on preparing for class assemblies and other performances. Get them to draw up a list of common-sense rules for preparing a presentation, bearing in mind the contrast of approach between Charlie and Alex.

Remind the children about the assembly idea in which a group designed a sitting throw competition for sports day, and ask them to write or improvise a short drama on the same theme to share with the class later.

Kinaesthetic ideas

The children could conduct a survey within the class, asking questions about how and where they like to do their homework. Questions could include references to where, when, whether they like to have TV or music on when they're working and so on. Graphs could then be drawn to show the results and share them with the rest of the class.

Tactile ideas

When Jesus told the original story, he said that the foundation for life was obedience to his words. Perhaps his greatest commandment was to love others—the basis on which most Christians make ethical decisions. The children could use a square-based pyramid net to construct a mobile for Charlie to hang from his ceiling. On the base could be written 'Love', with four other words or pictures of actions on the other four sides.

Group ideas

Split the class into groups and choose one person from each group to come to the front, where the teacher gives them a word or phrase to mime or draw for their group (the children could decide which they are more comfortable with). The words used could be from the story, or based on activities with 'love' as a foundation. Examples could be:

sports day
chart album
head teacher
laptop
birthday present
first-aid kit
helping hand
friendship bracelet

4

The best party ever

TARGET

The generosity of love; God's openness

The day of Daniel's birthday party dawned warm and sunny for a change. He rushed downstairs to check that his mum had made all the arrangements, and was pleased to find a smart cake sitting on the worktop, next to a pile of polythene party bags. Fantastic! He couldn't wait. No school today because it was Saturday, and he knew the time would drag terribly up to three o'clock when the party was due to start. He supposed that fetching a DVD film from the hire shop would take some time, but even that would leave ages to fill.

Mum suggested that his room could do with a tidy, and of course there was his new computer game to try out, but by two o'clock he was pacing up and down in the living-room.

'Why don't you go and call for 'em?' murmured Mum from the sofa, where she was trying to snatch a brief nap before the party guests descended. 'They all live on the estate, don't they?'

This was true, so, grabbing his baseball cap, Daniel slipped excitedly out of the front door and up the garden path, clanging the gate noisily behind him. He would call on Katie first. She lived nearest and she'd help him to persuade the others to come a bit earlier than they'd planned. Everybody always did what Katie said, or else. When he reached her house, he was pleased to see that she was playing in the front garden, although he wasn't sure at first exactly what she was doing.

As he rounded the privet hedge and placed his hand on the gate handle, he suddenly found out, as a bouncy bundle wrapped in black and tan rushed across to greet him with a mixture of warm tongue, sharp little teeth and exuberant barking. It was a fantastic Rottweiler puppy, just like the one Katie had always said she was going to get one day. So she'd finally done it. Great!

'I've come to collect you for the party,' called Daniel over the noise of the bounding creature beyond the gate. 'Mum says we can start early.'

Katie's face changed from that of a proud new owner to a disappointed friend in an instant.

'Oh, sorry Danny,' she mumbled, her gaze dropping awkwardly to the crazy paving at her feet. 'I've got to take Spike to the vet's for his injections and then we're off to the beach to give him a run. I only got him last night and I want to try him out. I was going to ring you, honest…'

'No problem. It's only a birthday party,' said Daniel, trying hard to keep the disappointment out of his voice. 'P'raps I'll see you tomorrow.'

He turned slowly away, trying hard to ignore the now irritating sound of Spike and Katie tugging fiercely against each other with an old trainer. Next stop, Ben. He'd be up for it.

It was less than five minutes later that Daniel was standing at Ben's front door, panting heavily from the exertion of running. He pressed the doorbell confidently and stood back expectantly as he watched Ben's mum approaching.

'I've come for Ben,' announced Daniel when she had opened the door. 'Mum says we can start when we're ready.'

'I'm afraid you've just missed him, Danny. He's just gone out on his new mountain bike. You know—the one he's been saving up for since Christmas. His dad took him to collect it this morning. He told me to tell you if you called. He said you wouldn't mind if he missed the party.'

Ben's mum didn't seem too convinced about this last bit, but Daniel smiled as positively as he could, swallowed the uncomfortable lump that had suddenly risen into his throat, and turned away with as cheerful a wave as he could manage.

Never mind, he thought. Ryan would be OK. As Daniel's best friend since nursery, there was no way he'd let him down… was there?

A short walk later, Daniel hesitantly raised his arm to knock twice on the thick white plastic of Ryan's front door. Ryan opened it, dressed in his favourite football shirt, denim jacket and jeans. His gelled hair was carefully arranged in soggy spikes, a certain sign that he was ready to go out. Daniel grinned with relief, and was about to launch into his explanation when he noticed a disturbing expression on his friend's face.

'Dan,' began Ryan, avoiding his eye. 'If you've come about your party, I've got something to tell you. You know I asked Zoë out on Friday. Well, she rang this morning and invited me to the pictures. You know how long I've been waiting for this sort of chance, so you'll understand if I can't make it to your party, won't you? I mean, it's not as though I'm the only one coming, is it?'

Dan's mum knew from the look on his face that he was disappointed, but she couldn't believe what she was hearing when he poured out his story.

'What, none of 'em?' she shouted. 'After all the trouble I've gone to!' She sent Daniel straight on to the street, and to the playground near the shops. 'I'll go and get some more stuff, and you find the guests,' she said, pulling her handbag off the banister as she left the house with him. Daniel soon found some children from his class, people he'd never really taken the trouble to get to know before. He even invited some younger children from next door—children he couldn't stand, if he was honest. 'Why not?' he thought, if your friends could let you down so badly.

As Dan and his mum watched the last party guest walk down the drive that night, they exchanged tired but warm smiles. In spite of the afternoon's disappointing start, they'd actually had a good time. As Dan closed the door, he decided it had probably been the best party ever. Who'd have thought it possible?

(Find this story as Jesus told it in Luke 14:15–24.)

CURRICULUM LINKS

PSHE KS1: 1b share opinions; 1c recognize and deal with feelings; 1d think about themselves; 2a discussions; 2c recognize choices; 2d agree and follow rules; 2e needs and responsibilities; 4a behaviour affects others; 4b work co-operatively; 4c differences and similarities; 5b feel positive; 5c discussions; 5d real choices.

PSHE KS2: 1a talk and write about opinions; 1b recognize their worth, seeing mistakes, setting personal goals; 1e develop skills; 1h use and interpret information; 2d responsibilities and duties; 4a care about others; 4f differences and similarities; 5a take responsibility; 5b feel positive about themselves.

RE KS1: 1a explore religious stories; 1c belonging to a religion; 1d religious beliefs in the arts; 2c identify what matters to them and others; 2d reflect on moral values and their own behaviour; 3a Christianity; 3c a religious community; 3j belonging; 3k myself; 3p sharing their own beliefs, ideas and values.

RE KS2: 1a describe stories; 1f religious responses to ethical questions; 2a belonging to a religious community; 2c discuss religious belief; 2d right and wrong; 3f teachings and authority; 3k following a religion or belief; 3m fairness; 3o discussing religious and philosophical questions; 3p considering experiences and feelings.

MENTAL SWITCH-ON

Have you ever had to turn down a party invitation? When you think about your own birthday parties, which was your favourite so far? Why was it your favourite?

SO WHAT?

○ How do you think Daniel had chosen who to invite to his party?

○ What feelings might Katie have had to prevent her from ringing Daniel?

○ What do you think Ben's mum thought about having to tell Daniel that Ben couldn't come to the party?

○ How would you describe Daniel's feelings when he got home from calling for his friends?

○ What might have been the reasons that the party went so well in the end?

○ What do you think Daniel said to his friends at school the next week?

○ What might be good reasons for not going to a party, after you've accepted the invitation to it?

○ What are the five most important aspects of true friendship?

○ What do you think the story has to say about who might be invited to God's 'party'?

PRAYER

Thank you for the fun of parties,
thank you for the joy of friendship,
and thank you for the chance to share
all that we have with others. Amen

POSSIBILITIES

Visual ideas

Ask the children to design an invitation, perhaps on the computer, for a party they would like to hold, and to which they would like to invite a disadvantaged group of children, perhaps from central Europe, Africa or another area of the world which is in the news. (They could imagine that someone else would fund the travel costs.)

Auditory ideas

The children could improvise and write a dialogue between one of the guests and Daniel, set on the playground on the following Monday morning. They could focus on what Daniel had learned from the experience and the guest's reaction to the change in his outlook. Less able and younger children could simply describe an apologetic and forgiving scenario between the characters, or perhaps a frosty reception from Daniel.

Kinaesthetic ideas

Ask the children to design a board game on squared paper showing a possible route round Daniel's estate, including the houses of his friends and the park where his eventual party guests came from. Given a dice and counters, they could see who could make the journey most quickly, choosing their own order if they wish.

An extension could be to add a particular dice throw or throws to indicate whether the friend(s) can come or not (for example, an even dice throw on reaching Katie's house means that she can come; an odd throw means that she can't).

Tactile ideas

Try giving the children a number of cards, each having a characteristic of a good friend written on it. In pairs, they then have to think up and mime brief scenes that exemplify the given characteristic. When each pair has completed two words, the cards could be exchanged between pairs once or twice. The children could then choose one of the scenes to perform to a wider audience. Words used might include:

patience
encouragement
listening
honesty
forgiveness
support
belief

Group ideas

Put the children into small groups and provide each child with a copy of the local church's newsletter or notice sheet (or something from a suitable church website). Ask the children to cut out examples of 'God's party', showing how open the church is to others. They could place their examples in the middle of their table, noting which ones have been chosen by more than one person, and the relative merits of each in terms of demonstrating God's inclusive love.

A development could be to come up with a poster, as a group or in pairs, which advertises other church activities that the children can think of to welcome new people in.

The seed tray

Miss Davies had just finished reading the story, and everyone was sitting there on the carpet, basking in the warm glow that always followed a chapter of the chosen book. Well... nearly everyone.

'Tomorrow, we'll be starting our seed growing experiment,' explained Miss Davies, putting the book carefully back on to her immaculate desk. 'I'd like you all to go to your mums and dads when you get home tonight and ask them if they can spare any seeds. It doesn't matter what sort they are, but you must ask their permission first, of course.'

Earlier that afternoon, each table had meticulously prepared a seed tray with compost. As in all fair tests, the trays and the compost were identical, with each of the trays being filled to within a centimetre of the top. All the class needed now was something to sow in each one.

Amy couldn't wait to get home and ask either of her parents' permission to go into the greenhouse and rummage in the old ice cream tub that lived on the benching. It was always carelessly stuffed with half-empty packets of all sorts of seeds left over from previous springs.

Sam was equally keen to get home, for altogether different reasons. He knew where there was some seed too, but he had no intention of asking anyone about it. He would help himself, because he had a plan that he thought would spoil things for his table very nicely.

Next morning, the children drifted into the classroom chattering quietly to each other, many of them clutching assorted bags of seeds. Miss Davies had set the seed trays out on the tables so that they could make a start on their experiment straight after registration.

The children took out their Early Work books and set about that morning's maths and spelling puzzles, although rather distractedly in the case of those who couldn't resist playing with the seeds they'd brought in. Miss Davies went to each table in turn to help them set up their tray for the experiment. This consisted simply of sowing a row of each seed, watering the compost and then covering half of the tray with a large piece of black card.

Blue Table had to wait until last, but their teacher finally arrived and the fun could begin.

'Who's brought some seeds, then?' she enquired brightly.

Amy proudly pushed forward half a packet of runner beans, and Brendan produced some cauliflower seeds in a plastic bag. The other four, including Sam, wriggled in their seats un-comfortably, making various excuses as to why they hadn't brought any.

'Never mind,' added Miss Davies. 'These will do nicely.'

Amy and Brendan kindly agreed to share their seeds with the rest, and everyone had a go at placing the seeds in the compost in four straight rows, two of each vegetable, before Amy watered them in with a sprayer. All the trays were labelled, the cardboard added across each one, and then placed together on the benching under the window where the sunlight was strongest.

Everyone then settled down to the rest of the morning's activities. Well... nearly everyone. Sam was too excited to concentrate completely, because he had yet to put his plan into action. He must wait until lunch time.

Sam took his time eating his sandwiches. The dinner ladies tried to speed him up, but he managed to be the last one to take his lunchbox back to the cloakroom. He sauntered through the cloakroom to reach his peg, put the plastic tub and bottle in his bag, and then peered back into the classroom.

There was no one about, so he walked jauntily up to the seed trays, found the one belonging to Blue Table, and gently disturbed the surface of the compost with his fingernails. He then swiftly slipped a small bag out of his trouser pocket, scattered some seeds on to the tray, and covered them over with speedy, zigzag movements, before retracing his steps into the cloakroom. Looking briefly over his shoulder, he was relieved to discover that the classroom and the corridor were both still deserted.

It was two weeks later when the children began to notice significant changes in their trays. The seeds had germinated at different rates, although it was clear that in most of the trays the cardboard cover had not stopped the seeds from appearing. In fact, for some of the plants it seemed to have speeded up germination. When Miss Davies joined the children on Blue Table, she found them looking anxious. Amy seemed particularly upset.

'What's the matter?' asked the teacher, her voice full of concern. 'Haven't your beans come up yet?'

'Yes,' replied Amy, 'and Brendan's cauliflowers. But what are all these?' She pointed at a mass of little green shoots that had burst energetically through the surface of the compost all over the tray.

Miss Davies lifted the tray for closer inspection.

'These are grass seeds, I think,' she murmured. 'But how did they get in here? They can't have been in the compost or everyone would have them in their trays.' It was as she was saying this that a thought occurred to her. She glanced down at the faces of the children on Blue Table, and noticed that Sam's eyes alone were conveniently facing downwards, away from her gaze. 'I think I know what's happened,' she said. The edge to her voice made Sam look up in surprise, and as he caught her eye he realized that somehow she knew.

'Shall we pull the grass out?' asked Brendan, keen to remedy the situation.

'No. That would disturb the roots of the other seeds,' Miss Davies explained. 'We'll let them grow a bit bigger first, then we can transplant the beans and cauliflowers into another tray, ready for planting outside in the garden.'

Amy was feeling much better now that she realized the experiment hadn't been ruined completely. 'What will we do with the grass plants when we've taken out the others?' she asked.

'They can be thrown on to the compost heap in the wildlife area for recycling,' replied Miss Davies. 'That will be a nice little job for Sam,' she added with a meaning that, judging by the look on his face, was not lost on him.

(Find this story as Jesus told it in Matthew 13:24 30.)

CURRICULUM LINKS

PSHE KS1:1a right and wrong; 1b share opinions; 1c feelings; 2a discussions; 2c recognize choices; 2e responsibilities; 2h contribute to life; 4a behaviour affects others; 4b work co-operatively; 5a take responsibility; 5b feel positive; 5c discussions.

PSHE KS2: 1a talk and write about opinions; 1b recognize their worth, set personal goals; 1e develop skills; 2c consequences of anti-social behaviours; 2d responsibilities and duties; 4a actions affect themselves and others; 5a take responsibility; 5b feel positive about themselves; 5d make real choices; 5f develop relationships.

RE KS1: 1a explore religious stories; 1d religious beliefs in the arts; 2c identify what matters to them and others; 2d reflect on moral values and their own behaviour; 3a Christianity; 3j belonging; 3k myself; 3p sharing their own beliefs, ideas and values.

RE KS2: 1a describe stories; 1f religious responses to ethical questions; 2c discuss religious belief; 3a Christianity; 3e how beliefs impact on lives; 3o discussing religious and philo-sophical questions; 3p considering experiences and feelings; 3r expressing insights.

MENTAL SWITCH-ON

What conditions do seeds need to germinate? (Water, oxygen, warmth.) How many times have you grown seeds in a school science investigation? What do you do when an experiment goes wrong?

SO WHAT?

- Why do you think Sam wanted to sabotage the experiment?
- How might Brendan and Amy have felt when they saw the mystery plants growing?
- What made Miss Davies suspicious about Sam?
- How do you think Sam normally behaved in the classroom?
- What do you think Jesus was trying to say about good and bad in this story?
- Which character do you think represents God?
- Are there situations in everyday life where bad tries to overcome good?
- Why was Miss Davies' solution to the problem a good idea?
- What occasions can you think of when people have started something without knowing quite how well it will turn out?

PRAYER

Let us plant good seeds in our lives,
let us water them and care for them,
let us see them grow into something fantastic.
Amen

POSSIBILITIES

Visual ideas

Provide paints or other art media for the children to produce pictures showing the beans growing and the grass surrounding them. A bean plant might be a useful resource in season to help with the realism.

An extension for the more able might be to draw an imaginary and beautiful plant growing something 'good' in spite of being surrounded by darker, unpleasant imaginary plants which are trying to spoil its growth. A brief look at the work of Georgia O'Keeffe might be helpful (search at www.art.com, for example).

Alternatively, less able artists or younger children could produce a print version using seed heads, grasses, string and other natural resources.

Auditory ideas

Suggest that the children retell the story to each other in pairs, each pair working out a set of actions for the class to perform, which will help them remember the key points of the story. Pairs or groups could then share their ideas and prepare one or two performances for an audience of younger children.

Kinaesthetic ideas

Discuss with the children a worthwhile community project, perhaps tidying up the area around school, or adding playground equipment or other facilities. Then ask them to list those factors, such as vandalism, that could work against the project. The children could then draw up a snakes and ladders game on squared paper, showing the ups and downs as good and bad factors impacting on progress.

Tactile ideas

Ask the children to look at a selection of seed packets, noting the way the instructions are written. Then ask them to devise a packet for imaginary friendship seeds. They would need to consider what friendship looks like when it is fully grown, and then to draw it on the front of the packet.

As a parallel to planting and watering real seeds, the children would need to discuss in pairs or small groups what conditions foster a successful friendship and in what order. All the necessary information could then be included on a net for the finished product, which may be folded up and glued or displayed flat.

Group ideas

Find a piece of music that allows groups of children to produce a dance, incorporating the idea of developing something good in life that is then threatened by something bad. The objective would be to show good triumphing over bad. The children may need guiding through the ideas they could work on, so a class discussion of worthwhile projects and the things that threaten their success might be a useful starting point.

The lunch-time helpers

TARGET

Being prepared

It had been a very long term, and Class Four's room was what the head teacher Mrs Presley would have called 'a shambles', had she seen it lately. Fortunately for Mrs Evans, the class teacher, she had not visited for a while, but clearly the situation could not go on for much longer. Mrs Evans therefore decided to spend the next few lunch times having a good tidy up. For that, she realized that she would need help—quite a lot of help, actually. With this in mind, she addressed the class just before they went to the cloakroom to wash their hands and visit the toilet.

'Would anyone like to come back to the classroom after they've had lunch?' she asked wearily, surveying the mess around her as she did so. A stack of paint pots towered over the sink, all of them that stubborn, unpleasant purple colour which always seemed to develop on palettes and water tubs alike, given enough time.

The bookshelves were untidy; labels were hanging off trays; dice, counting cubes and tape measures were jumbled willy-nilly into the wrong trays in the maths corner; the paper cupboard was spewing out pieces of all colours and sizes on to the floor; the cupboard door wouldn't close because of all the half-finished junk models that packed the floor, and every surface in the room had a pile of some sort of completed work on it.

Thirty pairs of eyes returned to gaze sympathetically at Mrs Evans, although only ten hands went up in solidarity.

'Oh, you are good,' she responded, overjoyed at their obvious support. 'Take a card each for the dinner ladies so that they'll let you in when I come for you. Look out for me on the playground, please. I'll come out around 12.30, which should give us about half an hour. I'll find a nice treat for you all for being so helpful,' she added, looking thoughtfully at a large jar of lollipops on the windowsill as she did so.

Mrs Evans handed each of the ten volunteers a laminated yellow card bearing the words 'Lunch-time Job', and reminded them to watch out for her at the appointed time.

Some time later, their lunches safely negotiated, ten children huddled together on the windswept playground, watching the door fixedly for signs of an emerging teacher. It was Lauren's idea to go and join in with the football game that was going on noisily at one side of the playground.

'It can't do any harm,' she explained. 'We'll still see Miss when she comes out, and then we can stop.'

'But what if you don't see her?' wondered Peter. 'She won't have time to wait, and she'll be dead disappointed if we're not ready.'

In spite of Peter's concerns, Lauren and four others decided to put their cards under the pile of coats that marked the nearest goalpost, and keep themselves occupied until Mrs Evans showed up.

Peter and the other four continued to wait, well beyond the expected time. Mrs Evans had probably got talking in the staff room. They knew what she was like, but even so, surely she would come soon. It was at this moment, 12.40 exactly, that a jaunty and rather out-of-breath face appeared at the door and beckoned them in. As quickly as she had appeared, Mrs Evans was gone, leaving the children to explain to a sceptical Mrs Sergeant, the senior dinner lady, what they had to do.

'Where are your cards?' she asked, almost severely—but then, rules are rules. Peter and the rest of his vigilant group waved their yellow cards triumphantly, and filed past Mrs Sergeant into the school, politely thanking her as they did so.

As the last of them trooped through the door, Lauren happened to look up from the free kick she was about to take. Realizing what had happened, she ran immediately towards the door, calling to the other four footballers as she did so.

'We're with them,' she gasped as she tried to duck through the door, but Mrs Sergeant moved firmly to block her path, arms folded in an unspoken challenge.

'In that case, you'll have cards,' she said quietly, smiling at the small group that had assembled as she spoke.

After a few seconds of searching, Lauren remembered where they were. One of the boys was despatched to collect them from under the goalpost, but he came back quite quickly with the news that they'd gone.

'Back in a minute,' said Lauren swiftly, and she slipped round the corner to the classroom window, where she managed to get Peter's attention by tapping quietly. She mouthed at him, asking to borrow the cards, but was soon told that Mrs Evans had collected them in.

'She's gone to the office to take a phone call,' he mimed back at her. 'You'll have to go and see her.'

Lauren hurried back to her group and they headed off towards the main entrance, hoping to persuade the dinner lady there to let them in to see Mrs Evans in the office. However, they had no sooner gone than their teacher appeared once again at the playground door. She glanced briefly across the busy playground, shook her head disappointedly, and returned to her classroom.

At ten to one, Lauren and her footballers finally reached the classroom door, with Mrs Sergeant doggedly marching at their heels.

'Where have you been?' asked Mrs Evans, looking up from the sink. 'I thought you'd be waiting for me.'

'Oh, so you were expecting them, then, Mrs Evans,' Mrs Sergeant confirmed with surprise. 'I would have let them in,' she elaborated, 'but these five didn't have cards.'

'In that case they can wait for another time,' said Mrs Evans. 'If there is one.'

Lauren and the others weren't certain, of course, but they thought there was every chance that they would have another opportunity to help out before the end of the year.

(Find this story as Jesus told it in Matthew 25:1–13.)

CURRICULUM LINKS

PSHE KS1: 1b share opinions; 1e set goals; 2c recognize choices; 2d rules; 2e responsibilities; 2h contribute to life; 4b work co-operatively; 5a take responsibility; 5b feel positive; 5c discussions.

PSHE KS2: 1a talk and write about opinions; 1b recognize their worth, set personal goals; 1e develop skills; 2b rules and laws; 2d responsibilities and duties; 5a take responsibility; 5b feel positive about themselves; 5f develop relationships.

RE KS1: 1a explore religious stories; 1d religious beliefs in the arts; 2c identify what matters to them and others; 2d reflect on moral values and their own behaviour; 3j belonging; 3k myself; 3p sharing their own beliefs, ideas and values.

RE KS2: 1a describe stories; 1f religious responses to ethical questions; 2c discuss religious belief; 3o discussing religious and philosophical questions; 3p considering experiences and feelings.

MENTAL SWITCH-ON

How do you feel about lunch-time breaks? Would you rather stay in or go outside? What activities would you like to do if you could stay inside more? What do you most like about going outside? How do you feel about football or other ball games on the playground?

SO WHAT?

- Who do you think should be responsible for how tidy a classroom is?

- What could you do to take more responsibility for the space you work in?
- Why do you think Lauren decided to play football while she was waiting?
- Why did Peter stay by the door?
- Why do you think Mrs Sergeant didn't believe Lauren and the others when they tried to go into school?
- Is it ever right to make judgments about people based on what they've done in the past?
- How important is it to keep promises?
- What do you think it means to 'practise what you preach'?
- What does the story say about the way Jesus thought people should behave?

PRAYER

When others need help, may we be willing.
When the time is right, may we be ready.
When we hear your voice, may we listen.
Amen

POSSIBILITIES

Visual ideas

The children could draw a plan of their classroom and designate each area to be the responsibility of a group or individual to keep tidy. Ask them to draw up a list of lunch-time rules, or to produce a one-page guide of tips to getting on with lunch-time supervisors, complete with a central picture of a smiling dinner lady. The more able could use a computer to design a card for use by their class teacher at lunch time.

Auditory ideas

Ask groups of children to act a favourite scene from the story. A development for the more able might be to write a dialogue between

Mrs Sergeant and one of the children, based on an incident from the next lunch break. Some children could work out a rap to perform to the rest of the class, based on how to behave at lunch time, or how to be ready to help others.

Kinaesthetic ideas

Give the children a set of cards with hypothetical promises written on them. They should deal out the cards and then take it in turns to put them in order on a continuous line, depending on how important they feel each promise is. When all the cards are placed in a line, individuals or pairs could take it in turns to discuss moving one of them at a time until the whole group is happy with the order. They could then record this in a written form.

Tactile ideas

Ask the children to use a box of games equipment to generate ideas for some new games that they could play on the playground instead of football. They could work in pairs or individually to come up with a set of rules for their invented games. Other children could then try the games out from oral or written instructions.

Group ideas

Give each group a time of the school day, ranging from just before school to home time. Then ask them to produce between them a picture of a fictional incident where someone needed help, a brief caption to explain the situation (handwritten or computer generated) and a short account of how the person was helped, and by whom.

More able pupils could record the account in writing; younger and less able children could rehearse the incident to share orally at the end of the lesson. A display of this activity could be made by the children, based on a large analogue clock face.

The last one on to the bus

TARGET

The importance of inclusion

What a fantastic trip they'd all had. Nobody could remember going on an educational visit like it. 'Hypothesis' it was called— 'an adventure in science and technology', according to the glossy brochures. There'd been buttons to push, levers to pull, water guns to aim and interactive computer simulations.

Everybody's favourite had been the mechanical diggers: they'd queued for ages, but eventually Mrs Lenton had managed to organize all the children into having a go. Well... almost all the children. Liam didn't want a turn, in spite of everyone telling him how great it was.

'It's just like being in a real digger,' sighed Sam with feeling. His dad worked for a builder, so he should know.

'Who cares?' sneered Liam, hands thrust deep in pockets, a scowl decorating his otherwise uninteresting face. 'It looks boring to me, just like the rest of this stupid place.'

'But Liam, you're the only one out of the whole three classes who hasn't tried it,' wheedled Mrs Lenton, placing an encouraging arm across his skinny shoulders.

'Come on, you'll enjoy it, I'm sure,' she added, without any real conviction.

Liam shrugged her arm away irritably and stomped off towards the mining exhibition, muttering inaudibly to himself as he shouldered a couple of girls out of his path. Nobody was sorry to see him go.

After lunch in a bustling, noisy dining-room, shared with what seemed like at least eight other school parties, it was time to visit the shop. Everyone had been told to bring just two pounds, but even that small amount took ages to spend. It was so hard to decide whether to buy a rubber, pencil and sharpener set or a woolly bear with a bright red T-shirt carrying the words 'Hypothesis Science and Technology Park'. Or perhaps they should get that keyring torch. But then again, how could you not buy a plastic viewer that gave you a fly's eye view of the world?

Three classes took their turn to meander between the shelves, picking up item after item, only to put them back disappointedly as they realized they were not quite right.

'Just get a move on please, everyone,' begged Mrs Lenton. 'The buses will be here soon, and we've got a long journey on the motorway ahead of us.'

Eventually, the last of the children dragged herself away from the till, still uncertain about her purchases, but resigned to the fact that Mrs Lenton wasn't prepared to wait any longer for her to make up her mind.

As the two of them hurried towards the first of the two gleaming 53-seater coaches, Mrs Lenton noticed a huddle of teachers and assistants in agitated conversation. Arms were being waved, eyes were darting from face to face, and 'I knew something like this would happen' looks were being exchanged.

'What's the problem?' she enquired as she drew near enough to make herself heard over the babble of voices.

'It's Liam. He's not here,' answered Mr Richards, whose class

Liam was in. 'He was in Jessica's dad's group at lunch time, but he went to the toilet, then disappeared. I'm really sorry,' he continued, 'but I suppose I'm not too surprised.'

'Don't worry,' said Mrs Lenton encouragingly. 'If anyone's responsible, it's me. After all, I am the trip leader. I'll just ask the kids if they've have any idea where he is.'

While Mrs Lenton clambered wearily up the steps of the first coach, Mr Richards hurried back to the second. Having quietened the chattering children, some of whom were having a sneaky suck at their drink bottles, both of them asked the inevitable question: 'Has anyone seen Liam?' On both buses the two teachers were met with stony gazes, shaking heads and quizzical expressions.

'Why don't we just leave 'im, Miss?' suggested one boy from the back of Mrs Lenton's bus. His idea was greeted with a chorus of laughter from his mates, but they soon went quiet when they saw the look on her face.

She hurried back down the bus steps, checked with Mr Richards that his quest had been equally fruitless and then marched determinedly back into 'Hypothesis'.

Mrs Lenton checked the shop, the water zone, the space zone, the adventure playground, the ball pool, the dining-room, the toilets and the central arena. Nothing—not a sign. It was then that a thought struck her. It was a wild idea, but it was her last chance before she notified the centre staff, the police and goodness only knew who else. There was just a chance. She hadn't tried the earth zone yet.

Mrs Lenton knew where to look. She marched straight past the groups of children from other schools playing on the different activities or filling in their worksheets. And there he was, his back to her, totally absorbed with the controls in his deft, flickering fingers, his gaze focused on the mechanical arm beyond the glass. Liam had mastered the digger.

Everyone was surprised by the look on Mrs Lenton's face

when she returned to the coach with Liam beside her. They were equally surprised by the two large tubs of sweets that she'd bought in the shop on her way out, one for each coach, 'To celebrate,' as she'd simply put it. But no one was as surprised as Liam who, on climbing the steps on to his bus, was greeted by the applause of 49 children and three adults who, for the first time in as long as he could remember, were genuinely pleased to see him.

(Find this story as Jesus told it in Luke 15:4–7.)

CURRICULUM LINKS

PSHE KS1: 1a right and wrong; 1b share opinions; 1c feelings; 1d think about themselves; 2a discussions; 2c recognize choices; 2d agree and follow rules; 2e responsibilities; 2h contribute to life; 3g keeping safe; 4a behaviour affects others; 4d family and friends should care; 5a take responsibility; 5b feel positive; 5g moral dilemmas.

PSHE KS2: 1a talk and write about opinions; 1b recognize their worth; 1e develop skills; 2b making and changing rules; 2c consequences of anti-social behaviours; 2d responsibilities and duties; 2e reflect on spiritual, moral, social and cultural issues; 3e recognize risks; 3f resisting pressure to do wrong; 3g school rules about health and safety; 4a care about others; 4e challenge stereotypes; 4f differences and similarities; 5a take responsibility; 5b feel positive about themselves; 5g moral dilemmas.

RE KS1: 1a explore religious stories; 1d religious beliefs in the arts; 2c identify what matters to them and others; 2d reflect on moral values and their own behaviour; 3j belonging; 3k myself; 3o developing creative talents; 3p sharing their own beliefs, ideas and values.

RE KS2: 1a describe stories; 1f religious responses to ethical questions; 2c discuss religious belief; 2d right and wrong; 3f teachings and authority; 3k following a religion or belief; 3m human rights, fairness, social justice; 3o discussing religious and philosophical questions; 3p considering experiences and feelings; 3r expressing and communicating their own and others' insights.

MENTAL SWITCH-ON

What do you most like about school trips (educational visits)? Which have been your favourite ones? What are the top five rules for keeping safe when you're out of school as a group?

SO WHAT?

- Why do you think Liam said at first that he didn't want a go on the diggers?
- What happens in the story to show that he has strong feelings about something?
- What could those feelings have been?
- How do you think Mrs Lenton felt when she found out that Liam was missing?
- Why do you think Mr Richards wasn't surprised that Liam had got lost?
- Why might Liam have gone to try the diggers without telling anyone?
- Who are the most important characters in the story?
- Why did Mrs Lenton buy the sweets?
- What does the story say about what Jesus taught about God?

PRAYER

Thank you for opportunities to have fun,
thank you for chances to learn about the world,
thank you for all those people who help us to discover things,
and thank you for never giving up on us,
however much we ignore you.
Amen

POSSIBILITIES

Visual ideas

Ask the children to draw line graphs showing Mrs Lenton's and Liam's feelings, rising and falling from happy to concerned, relieved, lonely, left out and so on. These words could be used to label peaks and troughs on the lines. Less able children could use simple facial expressions in a series of circles to show how each of the key characters felt as time moved on through the story.

Auditory ideas

The children could discuss in pairs how Liam felt. They could prepare a dialogue between the two voices that he might have heard as he was thinking about going back to the diggers. One voice would speak about the importance of not being late, the dangers of being alone and so on. The other voice would remind him of the excitement of having a go on the diggers, the thrill of breaking rules and so on. A dramatic presentation with three or more children could be recorded on tape or video, or presented live to the rest of the class.

Kinaesthetic ideas

The children could make simple board games involving someone searching for someone who is lost. Some pupils could take the opportunity to come up with their own idea, while others might work from the story or a suggestion from the teacher. The game could be completed when the searcher and the lost find themselves on the same square.

Tactile ideas

Ask the children to take it in turns to leave the room while the rest of the group hide some simple everyday objects and give the seeker clues to find each object. They could see how many objects they can find in a given time. The group would have to come up with some basic rules as to where things could be hidden. These could be recorded in writing, along with the results for each participant in the form of a table.

Group ideas

Ask groups of children to produce tableaux from everyday life showing some people doing a familiar activity, while someone else stands on the edge, excluded for some reason. The rest of the class have to decide what the activity is, and why the lone person isn't joining in.

Suggest that the children come up with a small card that could be given to all pupils on school trips, explaining basic rules for safety when out of school. The rules could be agreed in a full class discussion beforehand, or by smaller groups if the children are able to do so.

8

The missing homework

TARGET

Forgiving others

'Settle down quickly, everyone,' commanded Mr Gallant. 'We've got lots to get through this morning.'

All around the classroom, children reluctantly finished their conversations about last night's television, put their card collections in their trays, or placed bulging pencil cases on their tables. Soon, every maths book was open and every pair of eyes was facing the whiteboard, where yesterday's literacy homework sheet was massively displayed as a reminder of what they could expect next from their teacher, before the maths lesson got underway.

'If one person in each group would collect up last night's homework sheets and bring them to me, please, I'd be very grateful,' said Mr Gallant. 'As you know, I don't like to exert myself too much. There's a football match on the telly tonight and a few comprehension sheets to mark will be a great help if it gets boring,' he added, grinning. No one was too sure whether he really meant it, but judging by the usual frequency of his mistakes when the sheets were returned to their owners, it was quite likely to be true.

'Who's not given theirs in, please?' he asked pointedly as he gathered the sheets into a neat pile by banging the loose bundle on his desktop repeatedly.

Mr Gallant's piercing eyes scoured the room, alighting eventually on the one hand that had been timidly, and not very convincingly, raised into the air. The hand's owner, Becky, avoided his gaze, concentrating instead on one of the seven rubbers that decorated the table top in front of her. It was rabbit-shaped, and she turned it over and over in her other hand absent-mindedly.

Mr Gallant sighed heavily and then asked the usual question. 'Where is it this time?'

Becky's gaze switched to the direction of the window, through which she began studying a solitary crow scavenging on the playground, before meeting the inquisitive stare of her teacher.

'Me little sister drew all over it,' she volunteered after some thought.

'You haven't got a little sister,' replied Mr Gallant, feeling suddenly tired even though the day had only just begun.

'No, I meant me mum washed it 'cos I left it in me pocket, and now it's all mush,' she said by way of an improved offer.

Mr Gallant wavered. There was no way of disproving Becky's claim, although he was almost certain she had fabricated it completely.

'If you give me another sheet, Mr Gallant, I promise I'll do it for tomorrow,' she wheedled. 'Honest.'

Her smile, one of the very few talents Becky ever displayed at school, was always very hard to resist. And Mr Gallant did want to get on with the maths game he'd planned. He also sensed that he was beginning to lose the rest of the class's attention.

'It's the third time this month,' he said, still thinking hard. 'I've really had enough of your excuses this time, Becky. You can do it at lunch time in here.'

'But I've got a netball practice, and we've got this really important match on Thursday. Mrs Lenton'll kill me if I don't go. Please!'

It was this last word, combined with the agonized expression on Becky's face, that finally decided Mr Gallant. Besides, he didn't want to let down Mrs Lenton by making her star goal-shooter miss a vital practice.

'Oh, all right,' he said, feeling suddenly generous. 'See me at the end of the lesson and I'll find you another one. But,' he added pointedly, 'I want it in tomorrow. Without fail.'

'Oh thank you, Mr Gallant,' replied Becky, glowing with pleasure. She'd done it again. What a performance! And she'd wasted at least two minutes of the lesson. It was going to be a great day.

Out on the playground at morning break, Becky was on the lookout. She prowled across the tarmac, looking this way and that until she spotted her quarry. Standing by the netball post, bouncing a ball absent-mindedly with her right hand, was Megan Turnbull. Becky sidled up behind her, tapped her on the shoulder and grabbed the ball that Megan had dropped in her confusion.

'So, where is it then?' barked Becky aggressively.

'Where's what?' responded Megan, trying hard to remember what her latest foolish promise had been.

'You said you'd bring that CD in for me to copy,' said Becky, unpleasantly. 'And I want it now.' The threat in her voice was unmistakable.

'Oh sorry, I forgot, Becky, but I'll bring it tomorrow. Honest.'

'That's not good enough,' Becky replied. 'So I'm just going to have to keep this ball. Anyway, I need to practise my shooting. Some of us have got a big game this week.'

Becky turned her back on Megan, aimed at the netball ring, and took a shot. She punched the air triumphantly as the ball dropped through the target with a satisfying swish against the net.

Megan trudged disconsolately away, wondering how she was going to persuade her mum to let her bring the new CD to school tomorrow. She didn't notice Mrs Lenton watching from the staff room window. Neither did she notice two of her friends making their way purposefully towards the teacher on duty.

'I can't begin to tell you how disappointed I am, Becky,' said Mr Gallant sadly. 'You've let me down, and Mrs Lenton. But most of all, you've let yourself down.'

Becky was standing in the corridor, hands clasped in front of her, eyes down and, unusually for her, mouth firmly closed. She knew there was no point even trying to get out of this one. She would have to do the homework at lunch time. She would miss the netball practice, of course, but maybe—just maybe—she would be allowed to play in the match. As she stole a furtive glance at Mr Gallant's face, though, she wasn't sure that even the smile would work this time.

(Find this story as Jesus told it in Matthew 18:21–35.)

CURRICULUM LINKS

PSHE KS1: 1a right and wrong; 1b share opinions; 1c feelings; 1d think about themselves; 1e set goals; 2a discussions; 2b simple debate; 2c recognize choices; 2d agree and follow rules; 2e responsibilities; 4a behaviour affects others; 4e bullying; 5a take responsibility; 5c discussions; 5f develop relationships.

PSHE KS2: 1a talk and write about opinions; 1e develop skills; 2c consequences of anti-social behaviours; 2d responsibilities and duties; 2e reflect on spiritual, moral, social, and cultural issues; 2f resolve differences; 2k explore the media; 3f resisting pressure to do wrong; 4a care about others; 4c effective relationships; 4d racism, teasing, bullying and aggressive behaviours; 5a take responsibility; 5d make real choices and decisions; 5f develop relationships.

RE KS1: 1a explore religious stories; 1d religious beliefs in the arts; 2c identify what matters to them and others; 2d reflect on moral values and their own behaviour; 3k myself; 3o developing creative talents; 3p sharing their own beliefs, ideas and values.

RE KS2: 1a describe stories; 1f religious responses to ethical questions; 2c discuss religious belief; 2d right and wrong; 3f teachings and authority; 3m human rights, fairness, social justice; 3o discussing religious and philosophical questions; 3p considering experiences and feelings; 3r expressing and communicating their own and others' insights.

MENTAL SWITCH-ON

What does forgiveness mean? When is it hard to forgive someone for something they've done? How does it feel when someone else forgives you?

SO WHAT?

- How do you know that Becky made a habit of not bringing her homework back to school on time?
- How would you describe Becky?
- What does the story tell you about the character of Mr Gallant?
- What do you think Megan thought of Becky?
- How could she have reacted differently to Becky asking for the CD?
- How do you think Mr Gallant felt about Becky when he found out about the CD incident?
- What might Megan have said to him afterwards?
- What was Jesus saying to his friends about the nature of God?
- How do you think he felt they should behave to each other?

PRAYER

You see the best in us, not the worst.
You see us not as we are, but as we can be.
You see our hopes, not our failures.
As you are to us,
so may we be to others.
Amen

POSSIBILITIES

Visual ideas

Ask the children to divide a page in two, and then draw pictures of the people who have forgiven them on one side, with pictures of the people they've forgiven on the other side. Older or more able children could label the pictures, and add a caption saying what has been forgiven in each case.

An extension could be for the children to write a diary entry for one of the characters in the story, concentrating on their feelings about the episode. Obvious choices would be Becky, Megan or Mr Gallant. A harder option would be Mrs Lenton.

Auditory ideas

Give the children a selection of instruments and ask them to compose a piece of music entitled 'Forgiveness', with contrasting elements to show the change in their feelings when their offer of 'sorry' has been accepted. The children could add some simple statements in the middle of their piece of music to show the sorts of things that can be forgiven. A performance of the pieces would make a good end to the lesson or the basis for an assembly.

Kinaesthetic ideas

Provide a selection of newspapers, one for each group of children, and ask them to cut out pictures or stories about people who have done wrong. They could stick the cuttings on a piece of paper, then draw lines joining the extracts to words that show those who might be able to forgive them, or to words describing how their victims might feel.

Tactile ideas

The children could make a mobile, using a piece of card cut into a suitable shape (triangle, diamond, heart and so on). On one side they could write the feelings that they might have if they do not forgive another person for something that person has done wrong. On the other side, they could write the words that describe their feelings when they have forgiven a person who has done wrong to them.

Group ideas

Ask each group to discuss the adjectives they would use to describe God, based on this story, and assuming that God is like Mr Gallant. A development would be for the children to say how they felt about what God is like. They might be quite creative here, drawing on other cultural influences or stories they have heard. Of course, at this point many will want to say that they aren't sure, or don't believe in God at all.

The lost daughter

TARGET

Parental love and God's forgiving nature

David trudged home from school, his games kit heavy on his back, and his mind full of the worry of the approaching tests. All the teachers said it didn't matter how well you did, as long as you tried your hardest, but that was easy for them to say. They didn't have to take the tests.

He lifted the latch on the cast-iron gate and crossed the front garden, rooting in his trouser pocket for the house key as he did so. David let himself into the hall, dropped his games bag just inside on the wooden floor, and proceeded first to the biscuit tin and then to the front room, where he lost no time in turning on the television before flopping on to the sofa with a huge sigh. That was where his mum found him about half an hour later when she came in from work.

'Where's Holly?' she asked as she hung her wet coat on a hook in the hall.

'Dunno,' replied David, his gaze still riveted on the cartoon he was watching.

'She's normally home by now. I'll ring her,' continued Mum to no one in particular.

Life hadn't been easy in the years since the children's dad had wandered off, and the weight of all the long hours at work, the careful scrimping and saving, seemed particularly heavy at the moment.

'Her voicemail's on, so I'll send a text. Come and start the tea, there's a love,' she said to David as her thumb darted backwards and forwards over the keys of her mobile phone.

David, rested from his heavy day of revision, sprang into action with as much enthusiasm as he could muster. He could see how tired Mum was, so he started by putting the kettle on, ready for a nice cup of tea.

By the time they'd eaten their fish fingers and beans, there was still no word of reply to Mum's text message, nor was there any sign of Holly. Mum rang the college, only to discover that her daughter had not been in to her hairdressing course at all that day. David could see she was beginning to get worried, a feeling that he was surprised to find himself sharing the longer they waited.

It was when Mum went up to Holly's room to look for her diary that she discovered the note—and the missing clothes. She passed the scrap of paper to David as she pulled a handful of tissues out of the box in the kitchen and went through to do the washing up.

'Dear Mum,' he read, 'I am sick of college and this boring town. I have gone to Manchester to stay with Louise in her flat. I will be in touch. Love you, Holly.'

David remembered Louise vaguely as one of the endless procession of friends his sister had brought back over the years. He seemed to remember that she'd gone to Manchester to take up a job offer last September.

'I wonder where Holly got the money from,' Mum shouted from the kitchen. David was pleased to hear that Mum's voice was almost back to full strength. Mum found out the source of Holly's funds when she checked in the money folder later that evening. There was no sign of the bankbook she'd been using for the last ten years, to pay in money for Holly. David's was still there, of course, with the same amount in it as Holly's—a little over two thousand pounds, which Mum had managed to put away by going without so many things herself. She wondered how long Holly would be able to make that last in Manchester, always assuming she managed to get there safely.

The postcard arrived about a week later. It was there on the doormat when David came in from school. Apparently, Holly was having a great time. She was sleeping on Louise's floor, the nightlife was great, she had made loads of friends even in this short time, and she was looking for a job. They were not to worry, it said. David put the card carefully on the radiator shelf in the hall for Mum to read when she got in, and began to empty the dishwasher.

Time passed slowly until the tests were finally over, and then, as the days lengthened into summer, the weather improved. David played out with his mates most evenings, so that he almost forgot about Holly. Life was easier in some ways without the constant bickering that had accompanied living with a big sister. However, he noticed that Mum was taking Holly's absence much harder. Every night he would see her gaze longingly up and down the street as she closed the curtains, but each time she turned away disappointed.

Mum was just finishing her tea when the doorbell rang one evening in October. David had made a promising start at secondary school, and they were about to go to parents' evening together. Who could that be at this time? Mum almost ran down the hall before wrenching the front door open. Holly stood motionless on the step. She'd lost some weight, and her clothes looked rather rough, but the same hesitant smile was there.

'Mum, I've been such a fool...' she began in a plaintive voice, but Mum stopped her with a glance, opened her arms and welcomed her into the most incredible hug either of them had ever experienced. The story was soon told, about the friends who had rapidly disappeared once the money had run out, about the stolen mobile phone and Louise moving in with her boyfriend, who'd had no room for anyone else. It was the awful job she'd had to take which had finally prompted Holly to make her way home.

'Go and have a shower,' suggested Mum. 'Get a change of clothes on and we'll phone for a Chinese.'

It was at this point that David came out of the bathroom. He'd been cleaning his teeth and sorting out his hair, ready for the trip to school.

'Who are you talking to, Mum, and what's that about a Chinese?' he asked. When he saw Holly, with Mum's arm still wrapped around her waist, his sister's eyes met his. David looked instead at his mum, anger flashing suddenly in his expression.

'That's great!' he shouted. 'Absolutely wonderful! All these weeks I've worked my socks off helping in the house, getting good test results, starting at a new school, leaving my money in the bank the whole time, and I haven't even been out for a burger and chips. And now *she's* back, we're having a Chinese.'

He stood at the top of the stairs, glaring at them both, although part of him was as shocked as they were at this sudden outburst.

'David,' Mum said after a gentle pause, 'you've been wonderful since Holly went off, and no one can ever take away the lovely time we've had together. But we're going to celebrate tonight because your sister might as well have been dead, and here she is alive. Holly was lost, and now she's found.'

(Find this story as Jesus told it in Luke 15:11–32.)

CURRICULUM LINKS

PSHE KS1: 1a right and wrong; 1b share opinions; 1c feelings; 1d think about themselves; 2a discussions; 2b simple debate; 2c recognize choices; 2e responsibilities; 2f simple groups; 4a behaviour affects others; 4b work co-operatively; 4c differences and similarities; 4d family and friends should care; 5a take responsibility; 5b feel positive; 5c discussions; 5f develop relationships; 5g moral dilemmas; 5h ask for help.

PSHE KS2: 1a talk and write about opinions; 1e develop skills; 2c consequences of anti-social behaviours; 2d responsibilities and duties; 2e reflect on spiritual, moral, social, and cultural issues; 2f resolve differences; 3e recognize risks; 3f resisting pressure to do wrong; 4a care about others; 4c effective relationships; 4e challenge stereotypes; 5a take responsibility; 5b feel positive about themselves; 5f develop relationships; 5g moral dilemmas.

RE KS1: 1a explore religious stories; 1d religious beliefs in the arts; 2c identify what matters to them and others; 2d reflect on moral values and their own behaviour; 3j belonging; 3k myself; 3o developing creative talents; 3p sharing their own beliefs, ideas and values.

RE KS2: 1a describe stories; 1f religious responses to ethical questions; 2c discuss religious belief; 2d right and wrong; 3f teachings and authority; 3o discussing religious and philosophical questions; 3p considering experiences and feelings; 3r expressing and communicating their own and others' insights.

MENTAL SWITCH-ON

Have you ever felt like leaving home? Can you think of five things you would take with you? Why would leaving home be a very unsafe thing to do? What might be a better solution to problems?

SO WHAT?

- How do you think Mum felt when she found out that Holly had gone?
- What jobs do you think David did around the house to help Mum while Holly was away?
- What do you enjoy most about life in your house?
- How could you help out at home more?
- Why did Mum look out of the window every night?
- How do you think Mum felt about Holly leaving home with her share of the savings?
- If you were unhappy, who would you talk to about it?
- How did David feel when Holly came home?
- What does the story say about God?

PRAYER

It's great to have a family,
it's great to have a home,
it's great to feel we belong.
But sometimes it's difficult,
sometimes we fall out,
sometimes people aren't kind.

When we feel alone, let us feel your love.
When we feel afraid, let us feel your strength.
When we feel angry, let us feel your peace.
Amen

POSSIBILITIES

Visual ideas

Give the children a postcard-sized piece of paper or card, maybe with a picture of Manchester on the back, and ask them to write a short card from Holly to Mum and David, explaining how things are going. Older and more able pupils might be asked to describe how she is feeling now that she is away from home.

Auditory ideas

The children could improvise and write a dialogue between Holly and Louise when things have started to go wrong in Manchester. It is probably at this point that Holly starts to realize what she is missing. The children could write a list of the pros and cons of being at home, either to help them with the drama or when they have finished their improvization.

Kinaesthetic ideas

Ask the children to look at websites on the internet that would help a teenager or child who had run away from home. Ideally, these sites should be checked by the teacher beforehand and hyperlinks added to a document introducing the idea. The children could then design their own poster for an imaginary organization to offer help to young people in this position.

Tactile ideas

Try giving the children a menu from the local Chinese restaurant, and ask them to choose a menu for the celebration meal for Mum, Holly and David. Some of the children could then share their work by reading their order into a toy telephone.

Group ideas

Give each group a large piece of paper and some felt-tip markers. Ask them to take turns to write down all the words that describe mums and dads as special. They could then write each word on another piece of paper with the words 'God is…' written in the middle.

An extension of this activity would be for the children to take each example of 'God is…' and talk about what it might mean for Christians, and how such people would feel about themselves or try to live their lives. Perhaps they can think of examples of famous Christians who might have been motivated to do certain things.

The maths investigation

TARGET

Application leads to success

'For your homework tonight I've given you an investigation,' announced Mrs Savage as she wandered between the desks handing out photocopied sheets to the class. The usual eye-catching illustrations decorated each piece of paper, as did the fancy fonts, but it was still maths. You either liked it or hated it, she thought. However, she tried her best to convey her own love of the subject with renewed enthusiasm.

'There are plenty of possibilities with this one,' she explained, 'and you can all do it at your own level.' She let her gaze drift across the sea of faces in front of her, noticing four in particular.

Kirsty was sorting out her pencil sharpener collection, Ashley was sawing at his pencil with the side of his plastic ruler, James was trying to make words using his calculator and Lucy, rather unpredictably, was already poring over the information on the sheet, hoping to make a start on the challenge she was being set. Mrs Savage was a little surprised to see Lucy so engrossed, but was equally pleased at the effect the sheet was having. She turned her attention back to the rest of the class.

'I'll give you one or two clues to get you all started,' she added, wielding the electronic pen expertly against the interactive white-board. After five minutes of sharing ideas and giving instructions, she got the children to tidy everything away ready for break, dismissed them a table at a time, and then hurried off to the staff room for a well-deserved cup of coffee and a chocolate biscuit.

At home time, Kirsty darted into the cloakroom to look once more at the party invitation she had been given at lunch time by her best friend. Well, she hoped she was still her best friend, although the arrival last term of a new girl from somewhere miles away had thrown the whole relationship into confusion. Kirsty was so focused on the contents of the bright yellow envelope that she didn't notice her maths homework sheet fluttering uncertainly to the floor, where a number of unidentified school shoes trod it into a dusty, crumpled mess.

When everyone had gone, and calm had returned to the cloakroom, Mrs Reardon, the cleaner, trundled out of the broom cupboard where she had been making the final adjustments to her overalls. She swept the floor meticulously, and shovelled the rubbish into a black bin bag, shaking her head sadly at the sight of the scruffy homework sheet as it slid into the darkness.

'There'll be trouble for someone tomorrow,' she observed drily to herself, bustling off into the classrooms to empty the bins.

Ashley was watching television when his mum came in from work. She suggested that he might like to do his homework before tea. He managed to find three perfectly good reasons why he shouldn't, but none of these impressed her, so he took himself off into the dining-room to have a go at his maths. Once he had retrieved the sheet from his bag and found a pencil, Ashley began the investigation. It was easy at first. He followed the instructions carefully and seemed to be getting the answers easily. But then it suddenly became much harder. Ashley cast his mind back to the end of the lesson but, try as he might, he couldn't remember anything Mrs Savage had said.

'How's it going?' wondered Mum, as she brought the cutlery through to lay the table for tea. She looked over her son's shoulder at the half-completed sheet, and asked him why he was stuck.

'Mrs Savage told us some extra stuff,' moaned Ashley, 'but I didn't get it really.'

'You mean you weren't listening,' translated Mum, with a knowing look. 'Still,' she went on, 'at least you've had a go.' Ashley put the sheet back in his bag, and resigned himself to asking for help in the morning. Or, better still, he could just pretend that he'd run out of time. That would do for Mrs Savage.

James reached home full of enthusiasm for the maths investigation. He managed to get himself set up on the floor in the front room, right in front of the sputtering gas fire, just as his favourite programme started on the telly. He kept one eye on the dramatic events unfolding on the screen while simultaneously wrestling with the calculations on his sheet. As the afternoon drew on into evening, the television held more and more of his attention so that, by the time his dad sent him to bed, his maths sheet lay forgotten on the carpet beside the sofa, and with it the remains of his interest in the project.

Meanwhile, Lucy was having a whale of a time. She couldn't remember the last time she'd had so much fun doing her homework. She'd found the first part of the sheet quite easy, although it had made her think, but the more calculations she did, the more fascinating the maths seemed to become. What really surprised her was that she found herself turning over to the back of the paper to continue with the number pattern she'd discovered, even though maths had never been her favourite subject—in fact, far from it. She'd always found it rather boring.

Lucy was amazed when her mum told her it was bedtime, and she really had to drag herself away from the work she was doing. As she was going to sleep, she imagined going into school in the morning to show Mrs Savage how much she'd done, and what she'd discovered. Somehow Lucy felt that the whole of maths was going to be different from now on—more interesting, more fun even. She could hardly wait.

(Find this story as Jesus told it in Matthew 13:3–8.)

CURRICULUM LINKS

PSHE KS1: 1b share opinions; 1d think about themselves; 1e set goals; 2a discussions; 2b simple debate; 2c recognize choices; 2e responsibilities; 2f simple groups; 2h contribute to life; 4b work co-operatively; 4c differences and similarities; 5a take responsibility; 5b feel positive; 5c discussions; 5f develop relationships.

PSHE KS2: 1a talk and write about opinions; 1b recognize their worth, set personal goals; 1c face new challenges positively; 2d responsibilities and duties; 2e reflect on spiritual, moral, social, and cultural issues; 4e challenge stereotypes; 5a take responsibility; 5b feel positive about themselves.

RE KS1: 1a explore religious stories; 1c belonging to a religion; 1d religious beliefs in the arts; 2c identify what matters to them and others; 3j belonging; 3k myself; 3o developing creative talents; 3p sharing their own beliefs, ideas and values.

RE KS2: 1a describe stories; 1f religious responses to ethical questions; 2c discuss religious belief; 2d right and wrong; 3f teachings and authority; 3k following a religion or belief; 3o discussing religious and philosophical questions; 3p considering experiences and feelings; 3r expressing and communicating their own and others' insights.

MENTAL SWITCH-ON

What's your favourite subject for homework? Where and when do you normally do your homework? What sort of things get in the way of homework?

SO WHAT?

○ What did Mrs Savage think was the best part about maths investigations?

○ How can you tell that Lucy wasn't normally very interested in maths?

○ What stopped Kirsty from doing her homework?

○ How could Ashley have improved his work?

○ What stopped James from succeeding with the investigation?

○ What was it about Lucy's attitude that meant she really got into the investigation?

○ What does the story say about how life with God could be? What does it say about how people should behave?

○ Life isn't a maths investigation. What really important things in life could you complete if you focused as hard on them as Lucy did on her maths?

PRAYER

Show us the way to go; show us what to do;
show us how to make the world a better place.
Amen

POSSIBILITIES

Visual ideas

Ask the children to paint a picture using maths symbols and numbers as patterns, choosing exciting or relaxing colours depending on how they feel about investigating maths. Alternatively, they could make a collage using templates of symbols and numbers to draw round on newspapers, magazines, coloured paper and so on.

Auditory ideas

Some people like to work with music in the background. Ask the children to listen to short sections of tracks from a number of CDs and score each one out of ten for usefulness as background music for a piece of maths homework. The children could record their results in tables or graphs. The top three tracks could be played to the rest of the class.

Kinaesthetic ideas

Discuss an area of real life with the children, an aspect in which they feel that success is important. It could be friendship with someone, completing a charity project, or learning a skill like playing a musical instrument.

Give the children a rectangular piece of card with 20 squares laid out on it in the shape of a trail, and ask them to design a board game with 'success' at the end. In some of the squares, they will write imaginary scenarios that either help or hinder progress towards the goal, with instructions to move backwards or forwards accordingly.

Tactile ideas

Give the children a weekly timetable and ask them to plan a time-table for homework, ensuring that they have a work–life balance. They could use cards with different school subjects and fun activities written on them, moving the cards around until they are happy with the result, which they could then copy down.

Group ideas

Find a piece of music that allows groups of children to produce a dance, incorporating the idea of starting an important project, and showing some participants falling by the wayside, leaving one person to complete the task. Clearly, the children would need to develop quite large physical movements to represent participation in some-thing like a maths investigation.

An alternative could be to show people trying to 'be Christ-like' in the world, allowing opportunities to heal, befriend, lead, support and so on.

The buddy and the bully

```
TARGET
The new order described by Jesus;
the nature of pride and humility
```

It was time for assembly, so Mr Richards asked the class very gently to put their Early Work books away and tidy their tables. When he got no response from anybody—except Chloe, of course—he repeated the instruction, only this time with a little more volume and a hint of irritation in his voice.

Chloe was pleased to see that the other members of 6R were now doing as Mr Richards had asked. As someone who never failed to do what was expected, the sort of behaviour that she so often had to put up with in class always disappointed her. She sat bolt upright with her arms folded and her usual 'Have you noticed me, Sir?' expression painted on her face.

'Well done, Chloe,' said Mr Richards loudly, hoping that this positive approach would encourage some of his more reluctant pupils to settle a bit more quickly. It annoyed Mr Richards that his class was nearly always the last one into the hall. The head teacher, Mrs Presley, never failed to fix him with a meaningful look as he took his seat at the side of his class. 'Come on, Sophie,' he added, looking in exasperation at his watch. 'How long does it take to put a pencil away?'

Sophie was about to answer when she saw the look on Mr Richards' face and thought better of it. There would be plenty of other opportunities to wind him up later in the day, and she was tired from last night. It had been very hard to get to sleep, what with all the noise from downstairs.

A piece of music by Mozart was playing as 6R trickled into the hall a few minutes later. Mr Richards was delighted to notice that they were the third class in. He smiled with satisfaction at Mrs Presley, who returned the expression with a tinge of surprise, but also of pleasure. She was always happy to see her fellow teachers achieving good results with their children. She noticed Chloe, sitting beautifully at the left-hand end of the back row, arms folded and face turned expectantly to the front. Sophie, by contrast, was slouched two places to the right, her hand held in front of her mouth as a telltale sign that she was talking to the boy next to her. He was doing his best to ignore her, and looked imploringly at Mrs Presley to do something.

'That'll do, thank you, Sophie,' she said quietly but forcefully. 'Well done, Chloe,' she continued, with real warmth in her voice. When all the classes had entered the hall, Mrs Presley turned off the music, moved back to her customary position at the front and launched into her usual greeting. 'Good morning everyone.'

'Good mor-ning Mrs Pres-ley, good mor-ning tea-chers, good mor-ning ev-ery-one,' chanted the school in reply. The assembly had begun.

Mrs Presley told a short story to begin with, all about a boy who had been bullied on the playground, before being helped by a playground buddy from higher up the school. The head teacher continued by talking about their own system of play-ground buddies, looking proudly across at Chloe as she did so. She considered Chloe to be a shining example of the role of playground buddy, having completed all the training and spent the last year and a half carrying out her duties impeccably.

Mrs Presley thought that the buddying system was one of the best features of the school. Certainly, nearly all the children felt they had someone to go to if they had a problem—someone who would really have time to listen, and who might have experienced similar difficulties themselves recently.

As she was talking, Mrs Presley remembered that Sophie had joined the scheme, but she hadn't managed to complete the training course, in spite of lots of support. It was a pity, Mrs Presley thought, because the responsibility would have done her good, and might have stopped her being quite so horrible to other children on the playground.

After the reminder about the playground buddies, the bright blue baseball caps with 'PB' embroidered on them, which would help potential clients to identify the buddies, and the list of possible problems they could help with, Mrs Presley invited all the children to sit quietly for a few minutes while she put the music back on.

'I'd like you to sit and think about the school,' she suggested softly, 'and your contribution to life here. Think about what you achieve here each day, and how much more you could achieve.' She hesitated for a moment, and then added, 'You can use the time to think about the world, about God, and about your spiritual feelings too if you like.'

Chloe looked around the hall, at the backs of all the heads before and beside her, and felt good. She knew that her spelling test record was second to none, her knowledge of her tables was perfect, and her prospects for the forthcoming tests were great. She had everything going for her. But above all, she thought about her role as a playground buddy. She looked down at the gold badge on her school sweatshirt and glowed with pride. She wasn't sure what else she could possibly do at school.

Next, her thoughts dutifully turned to the world outside. Once again, her spare time was taken up with so many activities, including helping her mum at the local hospice shop, that she really had to feel very good about herself. She basked in the feelings of pleasure this gave her, before turning her thoughts finally to God.

Well, what could she say? If he (or she, or it) existed, which she couldn't be sure of, then he (or she, or it) was surely very pleased with Chloe, just like everyone else seemed to be. 'Thank goodness I'm not like Sophie over there,' she thought with deep gratitude to whoever or whatever had made it that way.

Sophie, meanwhile, was experiencing very different thoughts. She wasn't proud of herself at all. She didn't *really* mind school, although she had never been any good at it. It was so much better than being at home, but somehow she always seemed to blow it, no matter how much she wanted the teachers and the other kids to like her.

She was dreading the tests because what little bit she knew or could do always seemed to desert her at the vital moment. She also suspected that everyone in the school would be glad to see the back of her when she moved on to the secondary school. She didn't feel as though she contributed anything to school, or to the world, and as for God, well… She was sure that he'd have no time for someone as useless as her.

Mrs Presley's voice drifted across the hall, accompanied by the sounds of Mozart's music. 'I'm going to say a prayer, and if you agree with the words I use, you can say Amen at the end.' One person in particular was listening intently as Mrs Presley continued. 'Help me to know that I need help to grow, that I don't know it all, and that you care about me even when I don't feel I deserve it.'

Even from the front Mrs Presley heard a resounding and heartfelt 'Amen' bursting with meaning from the lips of one of her Year Six girls. As she looked up fleetingly, to her surprise Mrs Presley caught a pair of eyes gazing expectantly at her; eyes that sparkled with joy as she smiled with encouragement in return.

(Find this story as Jesus told it in Luke 18:9–14.)

CURRICULUM LINKS

PSHE KS1: 1a right and wrong; 1b share opinions; 1c feelings; 1d think about themselves; 1e set goals; 2c recognize choices; 2d agree and follow rules; 2e responsibilities; 2f simple groups; 2h contribute to life; 3g keeping safe; 4a behaviour affects others; 4b work co-operatively; 4c differences and similarities; 4e bullying; 5a take responsibility; 5b feel positive; 5c discussions.

PSHE KS2: 1a talk and write about opinions; 1b recognize their worth, set personal goals; 2b making and changing rules; 2c consequences of anti-social behaviours; 2d responsibilities and duties; 2e reflect on spiritual, moral, social, and cultural issues; 4c effective relationships; 4d racism, teasing, bullying and aggressive behaviours; 4e challenge stereotypes; 4f differences and similarities; 5a take responsibility; 5b feel positive about themselves.

RE KS1: 1a explore religious stories; 1d religious beliefs in the arts; 2c identify what matters to them and others; 2d reflect on moral values and their own behaviour; 3j belonging; 3k myself; 3o developing creative talents; 3p sharing their own beliefs, ideas and values.

RE KS2: 1a describe stories; 1f religious responses to ethical questions; 2c discuss religious belief; 2d right and wrong; 3f teachings and authority; 3k following a religion or belief; 3m human rights, fairness, social justice; 3o discussing religious and philosophical questions; 3p considering experiences and feelings; 3r expressing and communicating their own and others' insights.

MENTAL SWITCH-ON

What do we mean by bullying? Where is it most likely to happen? Why do people bully each other?

SO WHAT?

- Why do you think Mr Richards tried to settle his class quietly at first?
- How do you think Chloe would describe Mr Richards?
- Why do you think Mrs Presley played music at the beginning and end of assembly?
- What sort of person would make a good playground buddy?
- What do you like about school?
- What do you think you are good at?
- Which of the two girls does the story suggest is more open to God?
- What does the story say about the way God feels about people?

PRAYER

May we think the best thoughts when it's hard to,
may we say the kind word when it's hard to,
may we do the right thing when it's hard to,
so that everyone may know how good love is.
Amen

POSSIBILITIES

Visual ideas

The children could draw a picture of the two girls' faces in the assembly, with a thought bubble coming out of each one's head. In the bubble they could add a phrase or sentence showing what Chloe and Sophie were thinking while Mrs Presley was saying her prayer. Younger children could write thoughts on sticky notes and fasten them on to large drawings of the two girls.

Auditory ideas

Ask groups of children to work in threes to develop a short scene in which two children have a disagreement on the playground and the third (the playground buddy) talks to them both in order to sort out the problem. In a mixed age or ability setting, an older or more articulate child might be able to handle this last role best.

Kinaesthetic ideas

Try giving each group of children a set of cards showing different examples of bullying behaviour. The children have to agree an order in which to put the cards, from least to most severe. A development would be for them to write on the back of each card what they could do in response to each behaviour.

Tactile ideas

Give the children a simple net that will fold up into a sun hat or visor. Ask them to decorate it with a logo and a catchphrase to identify the wearer as a playground buddy. They could then work out how to fold the hat up and design an adjustable fastening for the back, so that children with heads of different sizes could wear it.

Group ideas

After discussing the message of the story, ask the children to make a list of what makes people important in today's society. They could cut up magazines and newspapers to produce a collage of faces, with some groups ordering them in terms of their 'importance', while other groups use Jesus' gospel values to arrange the pictures the opposite way round, with the 'least' important at the top.

The perfect guitar

TARGET

Making sacrifices for something worthwhile

Isaac couldn't wait to go back to school after the long summer break. It wasn't the work he missed, although he quite enjoyed that. It wasn't his friends, because he saw them through the holidays anyway. It wasn't even the school dinners, great though they were. It was Guitar Club. Now that he was about to enter Year Three, he could join Miss Stamp's lunch-time guitar classes, and above anything else in the world he wanted to play the guitar.

As soon as the letters came out about clubs, Isaac hurried home, hoping that Dad wouldn't have gone off to work yet. Isaac lived just across the road from school, and he was determined to bring his signed form back straight away so that there could be no chance of missing out on a place. He flung himself against the back door as he twisted the handle, and dropped his bag in the usual place by the washing machine. His big brother Courtney was already home from the Comp: his boat-sized shoes were kicked off as usual by the dog's basket.

'Dad, Dad, I'm home,' screeched Isaac. 'Are you there?'

Dad's head appeared round the living-room door.

'I'm just off to work, Isaac. Your tea's in the fridge. It just wants microwaving.'

'Dad, before you go, can you sign this form about guitar club?' Isaac pleaded, holding out the piece of paper and a pen.

'You don't have a guitar, Isaac,' explained Dad impatiently.

'I know, but it says you can borrow a school one if you need to,' explained Isaac excitedly. 'Please, Dad.'

'OK, OK. Anything for a bit of peace and quiet,' answered Dad with a tired smile.

He signed his name on the dotted line and took his coat off the peg by the front door.

'See you in the morning,' he said as he slipped out, before biking up the cul-de-sac and off towards town. Isaac leaned on the doorframe until Dad was out of sight, then ran back to school with his completed form in one hand and a delighted smile wrapped round his face.

He found Miss Stamp marking the maths books at her desk in their classroom. She was astonished that Isaac had come back so quickly, but she'd only been his teacher for a week or so, and she hadn't yet discovered just how enthusiastic he could be.

'You're certain of a place in the club,' she informed him, putting his form carefully away in her top right-hand drawer. 'See you tomorrow.'

The following Monday lunch time saw the first Guitar Club of the year. Isaac joined eleven other children in the music room after eating his lunch at the first sitting. Miss Stamp asked everyone to get their guitars out, put their empty cases neatly on the tables at the back and sit on a chair in the semi-circle that she'd clearly laid out at the front.

'If you need a school guitar, help yourself to one from the side,' she said, smiling encouragingly at Isaac and two of the others as she did so.

They tried a few basic chords at first, with the more experienced players helping the newcomers. Then they split into two groups, so that Miss Stamp could concentrate for a while on the better players. Isaac strummed away at the strings of the guitar, loving the feel of its shiny wooden body against his chest. It sounded fantastic—just as he'd hoped it would.

He was allowed to take it home to practise, and he sat for ages that night in the bedroom, trying to get his fingers around C and G and F (which was really tricky), until Courtney finally said that he couldn't concentrate on his computer game with 'that racket' (as he called it) going on.

As the weeks went by, Isaac improved steadily, so that as Christmas approached he was able to play the chords to at least six different songs. According to Miss Stamp, everyone was coming on so well that she was planning to include them in an assembly in two weeks' time, when they could accompany one of the songs that the whole school was currently learning in hymn practices with her.

The school guitar was OK, even though it was slightly scratched, but it wasn't like having your own instrument, and it was at this point that Isaac decided to get one of his own.

'Why don't you have one for Christmas?' suggested Dad.

'That won't be in time for the assembly,' Isaac explained. 'And besides, I've seen the perfect guitar in the second-hand shop window—the one on Victoria Street. I just need to raise some money.'

He closed his eyes fleetingly, so that he could see once more that beautiful, sleek, varnished wooden body, with its contrasting light and dark colours, and its deep black fret board. He'd seen it last night on his way back from his friend's party at the burger place, and he just knew he had to buy it. But how was he going to do that? The price was £60, and he only had about £7 saved from his weekly pocket money.

It was then that he saw the advert lying on the doormat, on a piece of yellow photocopied paper.

'TABLE TOP SALE AT THE CHURCH HALL—£5 A TABLE'

Perfect. He could look through his cupboards in the bedroom, find everything he didn't need, and sell it. The date was the coming Saturday, so within five minutes he was climbing the stairs with a big cardboard box from the garage in his hand.

✪

There was a buzz in the hall as the school gathered for assembly. Everyone was talking quietly about the twelve children sitting nervously at the front, seated in threes around music stands with their guitars lodged snugly on their knees. The words for the song were on the screen.

Isaac looked swiftly up at his classmates, dried his sweaty left palm once more on his trousers, and prepared to play, his orange plastic pick gripped tightly between his right thumb and forefinger. A second later, he thought his heart would burst with the explosion of pleasure that he felt as they started to play.

Meanwhile, back at home, Dad was doing some tidying up. The boys' bedroom was in its usual early-morning state. The curtains were still closed, the beds were unmade, and various items of clothing were strewn across the floor. But what caught Dad's eye was Isaac's cupboard. He still hadn't managed to mend the broken catch, so the doors had swung open, and he was astonished to see that the shelves were completely bare.

Dad knelt quickly down and tugged in turn at the two drawers, remembering as he did so the unusual number of trips backwards and forwards that his son had made to the church hall last Saturday. Both drawers opened far too easily, to reveal… absolutely nothing. As far as Dad could see, out of all the toys, CDs, computer games and books that Isaac had owned, not a single one was left.

(Find this story as Jesus told it in Matthew 13:45–46.)

CURRICULUM LINKS

PSHE KS1: 1b share opinions; 1c feelings; 1d think about themselves; 1e set goals; 2a discussions; 2b simple debate; 2c recognize choices; 2f simple groups; 5a take responsibility; 5b feel positive; 5c discussions; 5d make real choices.

PSHE KS2: 1a talk and write about opinions; 1b recognize their worth, set personal goals; 1c face new challenges positively; 1e develop skills; 2d responsibilities and duties; 2e reflect on spiritual, moral, social, and cultural issues; 5a take responsibility; 5b feel positive about themselves; 5d make real choices and decisions.

RE KS1: 1a explore religious stories; 1d religious beliefs in the arts; 2c identify what matters to them and others; 3k myself; 3o developing creative talents; 3p sharing their own beliefs, ideas and values.

RE KS2: 1a describe stories; 2c discuss religious belief; 3f teachings and authority; 3k following a religion or belief; 3o discussing religious and philosophical questions; 3p considering experiences and feelings; 3r expressing and communicating their own and others' insights.

MENTAL SWITCH-ON

Have you ever seen something that you desperately wanted? Did you manage to get it? How did you do that? How did it feel if you weren't able to get it?

SO WHAT?

- How did Isaac feel about starting Guitar Club?
- What did he do to show how committed he was to getting a place at the club?
- What advice do you think Miss Stamp gave the new guitar players?
- How can you tell that Isaac was keen to get his own guitar?
- What have you had to sacrifice (give up) in order to concentrate on something very important to you?
- When Jesus told the original story, he was saying that living life his way was like 'getting the guitar'. What might someone have to give up to do that?
- Is there anything you would really like to do?
- What things do you do that really aren't important to you?
- Can you think of anyone famous who has had to make sacrifices to be successful?

PRAYER

Give us the eyes to see,
the ears to hear,
and the mind to know
what's important in life.
Amen

POSSIBILITIES

Visual ideas

Ask the children to draw a time-line showing events in the story from Isaac's point of view. They could add drawings of his facial expression at key points in the narrative. Older or more able children could write a diary entry to fit with particular parts of the story: for example, after the first club meeting, when he had bought the guitar, and after the assembly.

Auditory ideas

Get pairs of children to talk about what one thing they would keep if they had to sell everything else to raise money for something they really wanted or needed. They could then draw or paint a picture of that one possession and talk about it to the class, explaining why they would keep it.

Kinaesthetic ideas

Give each child a target shape made up from concentric circles. Ask them to write in the centre a dream that they have for the future (perhaps only one word, or a short phrase). Then ask them to write in each of the other circles something that they would have to do, or to give up, to make their dream a reality.

Tactile ideas

The children could imagine that they are going to a table-top sale. Using price tags made from pieces of folded card, they could write down or draw ten of their own toys, games, CDs and so on, and add a price for each one. The children could then lay them out on their table and have a mock sale where everyone in the class is given a certain amount of imaginary money to spend.

Group ideas

Ask each group to decide on a charity, then come up with one possession they would be prepared to donate. Older children could write a letter for parents explaining the plan, and the class could organize a table-top sale in the classroom. For younger children, the teacher could produce a note and organize the event, perhaps for just one charity.

The son and the daughter

TARGET

Keeping promises; avoiding hypocrisy

It was Saturday morning, and Mum had just completed her usual tour of the house collecting dirty washing, first from the washbasket and then from a variety of bedroom floors. Having filled the washing machine and started its cycle, she burst into the front room where Harry and Beth were busy watching cartoons on the television. Harry was sprawled across the sofa, slurping his way hungrily through a bowl of chocolate cereal, and his sister Beth, two years younger, was chomping noisily at an apple.

'Have you seen the state of your rooms, you two?' demanded Mum, hands firmly on hips, eyes wide with irritation.

Keeping his eyes fixed firmly on the television screen, where the latest bunch of aliens was heavily involved in clashing combat with the robot heroes, Harry nodded.

'It's OK, Mum, I'll sort it out later.'

Beth looked at her mum, swallowed a mouthful of apple, and said, 'Me too.'

These two answers failed to impress Mum, who marched across the room, pressed the 'power' button smartly, and then turned round to her startled children.

'It's not good enough,' she continued. 'I've been far too soft on you two, but it's got to change. Right now.'

'But Mum,' responded Harry, swinging his long legs round on to the floor, 'I've had a hard week at school, I've got two football matches this weekend and I need to rest this morning.'

'Well, you're not going anywhere until all the plates and dishes are off your floor, your bookshelf and desk are tidy and your computer games are back in their drawer,' explained Mum. 'And that hamster cage is filthy,' she added as an afterthought.

'I don't care,' answered Harry. 'I'm not doing it.' With that, he stood up and stomped out of the room, slamming the door behind him.

The front room was very quiet after Harry's departure. Mum and Beth exchanged a long look, surprised by Harry's behaviour. Perhaps the move to secondary school had affected him more than they'd thought. Maybe things weren't going as well as he claimed. And there was no denying that football did take a lot out of him sometimes. Beth smiled supportively at Mum.

'My room isn't that bad, is it?' she wheedled, trying to reduce Mum's stress levels slightly.

'You need to tidy your soft toys, put your clean clothes away from last week and do something with your CDs. They're all over the place. And why don't you use that lovely jewellery box Nana got you for Christmas? There's stuff everywhere.'

'OK, Mum, I'll do it when the cartoon's over. Can I turn it back on?'

Mum nodded wearily and left the room with a sigh, turning her thoughts to the shopping and cleaning that still had to be done before lunch. She picked up the car keys from the shelf above the radiator in the hall, grabbed a coat from the cupboard by the front door and set off for the supermarket.

When Mum returned an hour later, the house was very quiet. On the dresser inside the front door she found a hastily scrawled note from Beth, saying that her best friend had called and they'd gone into town together. She assumed that Harry had gone to his football match. It was a home game today, so he would have walked down to the recreation ground with two of his mates who lived nearby.

Mum carried the heavy bags through to the kitchen and put the kettle on so that she could have a nice mug of tea when she'd finished putting the shopping away. When the last item was on the shelves, and the empty bags had been shoved into the overflowing cupboard under the sink, Mum paused to catch her breath.

'I'll just go upstairs and have a look at their rooms,' she said to herself, 'before I put my feet up with the newspaper and a drink.'

Beth's door had a sign on it saying 'Beth's room, Keep out, Especially Harry'. Mum eased the door handle down and went in expectantly. The curtains were still closed, so she drew them back and surveyed the scene. Nothing had changed. Well, actually, it had, because Beth's pyjamas were now strewn across the floor to add to the considerable amount of clutter that was already there—not to mention the clothes she'd taken out and then decided not to wear to town. They were hanging out of the chest of drawers, looking crumpled and sad at their rejection.

Full of anger and disappointment, Mum stormed across the landing and through the door to Harry's room, hardly noticing the 'Home Team Changing Room' sign fixed to it. Once inside, she stopped, mouth open in disbelief. She had never seen the room look so good. How on earth had he managed to do it in the short time he'd had? Everything was in its place—bed tidily made, curtains fastened back properly, bin emptied, carpet hoovered, hamster cleaned out. The window had even been left slightly open to help the smell of sweaty feet to disperse. On the desk, on top of an orderly pile of schoolbooks, Mum spotted another note.

'Dear Mum, I know I take you for granted, but thanks for

everything. I will try to keep my room like this from now on. Love, Harry.'

Mum walked back downstairs with the note in her hand and a warm glow in her heart. They weren't bad kids at all really, and it made the struggle of being a parent worthwhile when you got that sort of message. As she sat in the front room five minutes later, reading her paper and sipping her tea, Mum felt great. Still, she'd make sure that Beth would get her room sorted the minute she set foot in the house. That was a promise.

(Find this story as Jesus told it in Matthew 21:28–31.)

CURRICULUM LINKS

PSHE KS1: 1a right and wrong; 1b share opinions; 1c feelings; 1d think about themselves; 1e set goals; 2a discussions; 2b simple debate; 2c recognize choices; 2e responsibilities; 2f simple groups; 2h contribute to life; 4a behaviour affects others; 4b work co-operatively; 4d family and friends should care; 5a take responsibility; 5f develop relationships.

PSHE KS2: 1a talk and write about opinions; 1b recognize their worth, set personal goals; 1c face new challenges positively; 1e develop skills; 2c consequences of anti-social behaviours; 2d responsibilities and duties; 2e reflect on spiritual, moral, social, and cultural issues; 4a care about others; 4c effective relationships; 4e challenge stereotypes; 5a take responsibility; 5b feel positive about themselves; 5f develop relationships.

RE KS1: 1a explore religious stories; 1c belonging to a religion; 1d religious beliefs in the arts; 2c identify what matters to them and others; 2d reflect on moral values and their own behaviour; 3j belonging; 3k myself; 3o developing creative talents; 3p sharing their own beliefs, ideas and values.

RE KS2: 1a describe stories; 1f religious responses to ethical questions; 2c discuss religious belief; 2d right and wrong; 3f teachings and authority; 3k following a religion or belief; 3o discussing religious and philosophical questions; 3p considering experiences and feelings; 3r expressing and communicating their own and others' insights.

MENTAL SWITCH-ON

What promises have you made lately? Did you manage to keep them? How much does it matter that we keep our promises?

SO WHAT?

- Why was Mum so upset about the children's rooms?
- How would you describe the way Harry and Beth behaved when Mum came to see them?
- How else might Mum have dealt with the situation?
- Why do you think Mum chose this time to speak up?
- What feelings do you think Harry had, to make him tidy his room so well?
- Why didn't Beth do what she'd promised?
- How many things can you think of that your Mum, Dad or carer do for you in one day?
- Can you think of five things that you could do each week to help out at home?
- What do you think the story says about promising to live in God's way?

PRAYER

Promises, promises.
We all make them,
but we don't always mean them.
Help us to think carefully about our promises,
and to keep them if we should,
especially when they help others.
Amen

POSSIBILITIES

Visual ideas

Ask each child to draw a picture or plan of their bedroom at its most tidy. More able children could add arrows and labels describing who is responsible for putting things away, especially if the bedroom is shared with a sibling.

Auditory ideas

The children could work in pairs to discuss some basic principles for looking after their bedrooms, coming up with a bullet-point list to share with the rest of the class. An extension for more able and older children would be to ask them to decide what they could do on a daily, weekly and monthly basis.

Kinaesthetic ideas

Working together, the children could collect data from each member of the class on what they like to do as soon as they get home from school. It might work best if they came up with four or five alternatives in a brief discussion first, so that only a limited number of choices are available (with 'none of these' as a final possibility). Younger and less able children would clearly need support in producing the alternatives. Bar graphs and pie charts could then be produced from the data.

Tactile ideas

Given a piece of card, the children could design a bedroom door label that expresses their gratitude to whoever it is who helps them to keep it clean. They could add a piece of string through two punched holes so that the label could be hung on a bedroom door, and perhaps take it home.

Group ideas

Split the class into groups and ask them to work on a short piece of drama that shows someone talking about behaving in one way, and then acting in the opposite way later. The drama could include reaction from the other characters to what has happened. Of course, the teacher may need to prepare some scenarios beforehand for younger children. Performances of the short scenes could be used as the basis for a class discussion on hypocrisy, and the advantages of practising what you preach.

The bric-a-brac jar

> **TARGET**
>
> Knowing what's valuable in life

It was the week of the school Autumn Fair, and Miss Butcher had been asked to run a bric-a-brac stall. On Monday morning she came to ask Mrs Presley, the head teacher, what a bric-a-brac stall was, because she'd never been very involved with fund-raising before becoming a teacher.

'It's a stall where people bring their unwanted rubbish,' explained Mrs Presley, 'and it's basically for anything that doesn't fit on the book stall or the CD and DVD stall. You sometimes get some real treasures turning up,' she added, 'but don't hold your breath.'

'I think I'll get some of my class to help me,' Miss Butcher suggested, already picturing in her mind's eye the likely candidates.

When her class came in from the playground that morning, Miss Butcher told them about the bric-a-brac stall and asked for volunteers. She was very pleased to see that one volunteer was Jasmine, her arm thrust enthusiastically into the air. Miss Butcher chose Jasmine, Laura, Will and George, careful as ever to make sure that she matched the numbers of girls and boys.

'Please stay behind at playtime and we'll talk about what I'd like you to do,' she explained.

Jasmine was excited to discover that their literacy work

during the first lesson was about the Romans in Britain. History was her favourite subject. She loved looking at the past, and imagining the local area as it must have been many years ago. She found that if she closed her eyes she could almost see the people who would have been there at a particular time, walking about, working, fighting or whatever else historical people did. By far the best was when the teacher brought in real artefacts that you could touch or even smell. It was as if these objects unlocked a magical door into the past for Jasmine.

Today's lesson was no exception, because Miss Butcher had asked them to write a description of a Roman tile, borrowed from the museum. It had once been part of a floor, and the intricate patterns were still clearly visible on it. The tile was passed round the class, and Jasmine could barely contain her excitement as she waited for her turn.

At playtime, the rest of the class hurried out of the room, buzzing excitedly about the stories they were writing, with an imaginary Roman character who might have walked on the tile they had described earlier. Jasmine and the others walked up to Miss Butcher's desk, pulling up chairs as they did so. Miss Butcher explained that she would like them to spend Friday lunch time organizing the items that came in for the stall into groups, according to type.

'I thought you'd be good at organizing that, Jasmine,' she said encouragingly, 'because I know what a tidy mind you've got.'

Friday lunch time soon came, with the Autumn Fair due to start at three o'clock. The letters that had gone out during the week had brought in an absolute mountain of bric-a-brac. It was piled in a variety of bags and boxes in the corner of the hall, waiting for Miss Butcher and her team to lay it out on two tables.

'You make a start while I grab some lunch,' she suggested, disappearing in the direction of the staff room. Jasmine soon had everyone busy sorting, so that the tables were filling up in no time. Jasmine and Will decided which table each item should go on, leaving George and Laura to arrange the objects in a way that made them look most attractive. There were ornaments and vases, loads of soft toys and a number of very difficult jigsaws on one table. The other table had handbags, jewellery and crockery on it.

By the time Miss Butcher returned from her swift lunch, almost half of the objects had been placed on the stall. She wasn't sure that all of them really fitted the description of bric-a-brac, but if they helped to raise funds for the school then that was surely not a problem. Laura and George were sent away to have their lunch while Will and Jasmine continued sorting. Miss Butcher slipped off to find some sticky labels for pricing the items, promising to be back in a few minutes.

It was then that Jasmine picked up the jar. It looked very ordinary at first—just an old marmalade jar full of all sorts of odds and ends. She looked through the glass at the collection of buttons, brooches, curtain hooks and coins. It occurred to her to tip them out on to a saucer and have a closer look. When she did so, her heart nearly stopped beating. There on the saucer, half hidden by a couple of old pennies and a large pink button, lay a very old object indeed.

Tearing her eyes away from the coin, Jasmine saw that Will was busy trying to set up a car vacuum cleaner on one of the tables. She picked up the coin to examine it more closely, and found a man's head etched on to the surface. He seemed to have leaves arranged in his hair and he looked very cross about something. There was writing around the coin in capital letters, although the metal was so worn, and crusted in greenish brown material, that it was almost impossible to decipher any of them. However, Jasmine was completely certain of one thing. She had seen a photograph of something very much like this coin, only that morning, in a textbook about the Romans in Britain. She was also certain that she absolutely must have this coin.

Looking carefully around once more, she slipped it back into the jar, covered it with all the bits and pieces from the saucer and screwed the lid back on tightly. She was just tucking the jar on to the table with the ornaments when Miss Butcher bustled back into the hall.

'Thanks so much, you two,' she said. 'I think I can manage now. You go and get your lunch.'

Jasmine hung back as Will was leaving.

'Miss Butcher, I've forgotten to bring my money for the Autumn Fair. Can I go to the office and ring my mum so that she can bring in my pocket money?'

'Yes, I don't see why not,' answered Miss Butcher, 'but ask someone in the office first before you use the phone.'

And so it was that Jasmine was able to arrive first at the bric-a-brac stall, just as the Autumn Fair opened. There was the jar, hidden just where she'd left it, and it was with shaking hands that she handed over the 50p that the label indicated. When Miss Butcher took the money, she noticed the look of anticipation and excitement on her pupil's face as Jasmine grasped the jar with both hands. The teacher wondered what could possibly be inside the jar to make it so attractive, but she suspected that one day Jasmine would share the secret with her.

(Find this story as Jesus told it in Matthew 13:44.)

CURRICULUM LINKS

PSHE KS1: 1b share opinions; 1c feelings; 1d think about themselves; 1e set goals; 2a discussions; 2b simple debate; 2c recognize choices; 2f simple groups; 2h contribute to life; 4b work co-operatively; 5a take responsibility; 5b feel positive; 5c discussions; 5d make real choices; 5e meet and talk with people.

PSHE KS2: 1a talk and write about opinions; 1b recognize their worth, set personal goals; 1c face new challenges positively; 1e develop skills; 2e reflect on spiritual, moral, social, and cultural issues; 4a care about others; 4f differences and similarities; 5a take responsibility; 5b feel positive about themselves; 5d make real choices and decisions; 5e meet and talk with people.

RE KS1: 1a explore religious stories; 1c belonging to a religion; 1d religious beliefs in the arts; 2c identify what matters to them and others; 2d reflect on moral values and their own behaviour; 3j belonging; 3k myself; 3o developing creative talents; 3p sharing their own beliefs, ideas and values.

RE KS2: 1a describe stories; 1f religious responses to ethical questions; 2c discuss religious belief; 2d right and wrong; 3f teachings and authority; 3k following a religion or belief; 3o discussing religious and philosophical questions; 3p considering experiences and feelings; 3r expressing and communicating their own and others' insights.

MENTAL SWITCH-ON

Have you ever found anything valuable by accident? What did you do with it? What would you like to find if you could choose anything?

SO WHAT?

○ How do you think Jasmine felt when she first saw the Roman coin?

○ Why didn't she just take it?

○ What else might she have done with the coin?

○ If you had been Jasmine, who would you have told about the coin?

○ What kind of person must Jasmine have been to make Miss Butcher think she would tell her teacher about what was in the jar one day?

○ Jesus said that living in his way was like finding treasure, so what do you think the treasure in this story might represent?

○ What do you think the story has to say about how the followers of Jesus should live their lives?

○ Why was it important for the point of the story that Jasmine found her treasure by accident?

○ If you could choose one motto to live your life by, what would it be?

PRAYER

When I choose what to do, make me wise.
When I choose what to say, make me think.
When I choose what to be, make me strong.
Amen

POSSIBILITIES

Visual ideas

Give the children a piece of paper with a picture of a treasure chest in the middle, and ask them to draw lines coming out of it, pointing to between five and ten ideas that are important to them. These ideas could be represented by icons or written in words, and might be basic human rights or philosophies for life. A class discussion or paired talk might be needed to clarify children's thinking first.

Examples might be: treat others how you would want to be

treated, always help if you can, be truthful, always say what you mean, and so on. The Ten Commandments might be a helpful starting point (Exodus 20:1–17).

Auditory ideas

The children could improvise and write a dialogue between Jasmine and Miss Butcher, the week after the Autumn Fair. They would need to decide on the location, who brings the subject up and in what way they do so. Performances of each dialogue could be followed by hot-seating.

Kinaesthetic ideas

Ask the children to design a board game that shows characters going through life, doing things that are ordinary or inadvisable, but landing sometimes on squares that involve picking up a card showing a helpful life motto. The point of the game could be to collect one of each motto card to win the game, with cards lost for landing on 'negative' squares.

Tactile ideas

Give the children a white cardboard disc with a picture of a Roman emperor's head copied on one side. On the other side of the disc, the children could draw a picture of something they really value. It might be a possession, a person they love, or a personal quality they try to show in their lives (for example, kindness represented by a red cross, a smiley face and so on). The discs could then be hole-punched at the top and bottom, and joined together with cotton to make a mobile for display.

Group ideas

Invite a number of members of one or more local faith communities to come in and talk to different groups of children about what values they try to live their lives by. They may be able to explain how they discovered what they consider to be valuable in their lives, whether it was handed down from their parents or whether they happened upon it almost by accident, like the Roman coin in the story.

The sports day helpers

TARGET

The generosity of God's love

'It's Junior Sports Day this afternoon,' said Miss Savage at the end of the morning, 'and I'd like a few of you to help me put out the equipment during lunch time. You're on first sitting today, so eat your lunches as quickly as you can, please, and I'll come on to the playground to find you.'

As the children tidied away their books, pens and pencils, they eyed Miss Savage's sweet jar hungrily. She usually made a point of rewarding her helpers well, although she always insisted that these treats were not eaten until the end of the day, so that their recipients could clean their teeth as soon as they got home.

Sure enough, Miss Savage jogged on to the playground in her PE kit at exactly 12.15, spotting Alex and Anfal immediately. They were standing in readiness by the hall door, their empty lunchboxes in their hands, and were soon put to work carrying sacks out on to the field. The sun was beating down and the sacks were very dusty, not having been used since last year. Anfal felt a sneeze coming and pulled out her hanky quickly to smother it just as it arrived.

'Perhaps I'd better give those sacks a shake,' suggested Miss Savage considerately. 'Why don't you two go back to the PE store and fetch the net of footballs for the dribble relay.'

Alex and Anfal hurried back to the store and lifted out the net full of balls. They carried it between them, with Alex taking the harder option of walking backwards. He tripped on the kerb around the playground and fell over backwards, grazing his elbow in the process.

'Are you all right, Alex?' asked Miss Savage with genuine concern.

'Just a scratch, Miss,' he answered, dusting himself off and carrying on with surprising enthusiasm.

The two helpers continued their work on what was turning out to be the hottest day of the year so far. Miss Savage was very pleased that she'd remembered to put a reminder about sun cream in the letters to parents about Sports Day, and she hoped there would be enough shade for all the parents under the trees at the side of the playing field.

At half past twelve, Miss Savage returned briefly to the playground to choose two more helpers. This time it was Karanjit and Katie, both of whom had been playing on the tyre traverse. They were given the task of setting out cones to mark the start and finish of the various activities. They soon noticed how hard it was, working in a temperature of 27 degrees, but they didn't complain. Katie held the drawing that Miss Savage had given them, while Karanjit placed the markers on the painted white lines that the groundsman had sprayed on to the grass the day before.

Meanwhile, Alex and Anfal were struggling their way across the playground with a pile of hockey sticks and a bucket of cricket balls.

At a quarter to one, Miss Savage realized that the helpers she had chosen so far weren't going to have everything ready in time, so she turned her attention back to the playground and very soon saw Liam and Leanne sitting quietly in the shade.

'Come and do a job for me, please,' she called when she'd caught their attention, and they ran across to meet her energetically. 'I need you to fetch the skipping ropes and take them over to the far corner of the field,' she explained. 'Katie has a drawing showing you where they should go, so just ask her.'

The two went to the PE store and met Alex and Anfal, who were just leaving with a heavy mat between them that was needed for the obstacle course. Out on the field, Katie and Karanjit were putting the finishing touches to the markers, as well as laying out the small equipment in the lanes, ready for the competitors to use. It had been a great effort by them all, thought Miss Savage as she realized that they were going to be ready just in time.

After the bell had gone for the end of lunch time, the children all trooped into class, most of them heading straight to their water bottles for a refreshing drink. The Sports Day helpers were at the head of the queue, except for Alex, who, in spite of a rule forbidding it, had gone to wet his hair in the sink. When she had done the register, and when Alex had returned from his second visit to the toilets to dry his hair 'properly', Miss Savage asked her helpers to come out to the front of the classroom. The rest of the children started to get changed into their PE gear, while Miss Savage began to unscrew the sweet jar lid.

First she gave a packet each to Liam and Leanne, then the same reward to Katie and Karanjit, and finally a packet to Alex and Anfal.

'Thank you all,' she said with genuine gratitude. 'You all did a brilliant job.'

However, as they returned to their places, she couldn't help noticing that Alex and Anfal were muttering to each other.

'Is there a problem, you two?' she asked, a slight edge to her voice.

'It's not fair, Miss,' answered Alex boldly.

'We worked for 45 minutes in the hot sun,' added Anfal, 'but we only got the same as Liam and Leanne.'

'And they only did about ten minutes,' added Karanjit, who also clearly felt aggrieved.

'Hang on a minute,' said Miss Savage, putting the sweet jar down on the table rather more loudly than might have been expected. 'These are my sweets, and I'll give them out how I like. We finished the job and we did it well. That's all that matters.'

Everyone was very quiet as they carried on changing for what turned out be one of the best-organized Sports Days anyone could remember.

(Find this story as Jesus told it in Matthew 20:1–16.)

CURRICULUM LINKS

PSHE KS1: 1b share opinions; 1c feelings; 1d think about themselves; 2a discussions; 2b simple debate; 2c recognize choices; 2e responsibilities; 2f simple groups; 2h contribute to life; 4a behaviour affects others; 4b work co-operatively; 5a take responsibility; 5b feel positive; 5c discussions.

PSHE KS2: 1a talk and write about opinions; 1b recognize their worth, set personal goals; 1c face new challenges positively; 1e develop skills; 2d responsibilities and duties; 2e reflect on spiritual, moral, social, and cultural issues; 4a care about others; 4c effective relationships; 4f differences and similarities; 5a take responsibility; 5b feel positive about themselves.

RE KS1: 1a explore religious stories; 1c belonging to a religion; 1d religious beliefs in the arts; 2c identify what matters to them and others; 2d reflect on moral values and their own behaviour; 3o developing creative talents; 3p sharing their own beliefs, ideas and values.

RE KS2: 1a describe stories; 1f religious responses to ethical questions; 2c discuss religious belief; 3f teachings and authority; 3k following a religion or belief; 3m human rights, fairness, social justice; 3o discussing religious and philosophical questions; 3p considering experiences and feelings; 3r expressing and communicating their own and others' insights.

MENTAL SWITCH-ON

How do you feel about sports days? Which event do you most enjoy? Do you think we should have winners and losers at events like sports?

SO WHAT?

- Why did Miss Savage have a sweet jar?
- What do you know about Alex and Anfal's attitude to their work from the description of the way they set up the equipment?
- How did they feel about everyone getting the same reward?
- What might Miss Savage have done differently?
- What is surprising about the way the story ends?
- How do you feel about being rewarded for doing jobs?
- What are the five most important skills for people who are aiming to work well together as part of a team?
- What would happen if everyone was always given the same reward, however much they'd done?
- What does the story say about God's nature?

PRAYER

Thank you for the challenge of working,
the pleasure of finishing a job,
and the joy of helping others.
Amen

POSSIBILITIES

Visual ideas

Give the children a piece of paper with a clock face in the centre, showing the minutes of the lunch-time break in the story, then ask them to add pictures of the three pairs of helpers at the appropriate times. An extension would be to show the children doing each of the jobs they were given. The children could also draw the reward of sweets with each pair.

More able and older children might write a diary entry for Miss Savage, describing her feelings about the events of lunch time, as well as her thoughts on how the sports day went.

Auditory ideas

Suggest that the children work out a dialogue between Alex and Karanjit as they are returning to their seats. The dialogues could draw on the subsequent discussion with Miss Savage, or pupils could be given more freedom to be creative about things the two boys might have said that they could not repeat to Miss Savage. The dialogues could be recorded on tape or performed to a wider audience.

Kinaesthetic ideas

The children could draw a table of jobs around school and a different reward for each one. The jobs could be placed in order, from the hardest to the easiest, and the children could aim to match rewards to jobs. Finally, the children could decide one reward that could be used for all the jobs, regardless of how hard they are.

Younger or less able children could play a matching cards game with jobs and rewards already written or drawn on them. An interesting discussion might arise out of the unfairness of this approach, and the problems of getting people to do the difficult jobs if everyone is to receive the same reward.

Tactile ideas

Ask the children to design a sweet container, using a cut-out net, that could be used at their own school for rewarding children for some of the jobs they do. It might feature the school's logo, with a variety of words or phrases that emphasize the purpose of rewards and the satisfaction that can be gained from doing a job well.

Group ideas

Talk to the children about a project they could take on together within the school grounds. It might be an area that needs tidying, or, for older children, a piece of improvement work (for example, planting trees or painting a mural). Ask the children to plan the work out, to organize groups and to carry out their share of the task. At the end, all the children could share a treat of some kind, and write a diary account of what they have done, or perhaps what their feelings were about working together.

★ ALSO FROM BARNABAS ★

Through the Year with Timothy Bear

24 five-minute stories for special days and seasons of the year

BRIAN SEARS

Meet Timothy Bear, who, together with his family and friends, finds himself at the centre of many adventures guaranteed to appeal to young children.

The 24 stories in this book are ideal for use in collective worship and assemblies, PSHE and Circle Time, as an aid to the teaching of RE, or purely for enjoyment at story time.

There is a story for all major special days throughout the year, as well as stories for each of the four seasons, making the material an ideal resource to teach biblical and moral truths to 5–7s throughout the year. Each story includes a seasonal theme, PSHE links and Bible links, including the key passage in full. There is also follow-up material for the assembly or classroom, offering ways to help young children to get to grips with the story, express the story, own the story and live out the story.

ISBN 1 84101 394 3   £6.99

Available from BRF using the order form on page 127 or via the website, www.barnabasinschools.org.uk

★ ALSO FROM BARNABAS ★

Stories to Teach about God

12 modern-day parables with extension activities

SYLVIA GREEN

This book links Jesus' teaching in the parables to contemporary situations for primary-aged children. The pick-up-and-use formula has been developed after consultation with several primary school teachers and the material is intended for use with 6 to 10-year-olds in RE, PSHE and assemblies.

Bible text for each of the twelve popular parables is included in full. Each parable is then followed by a contemporary story to link the lessons in the parable to a modern-day setting. Reflections and discussion starters are given to help further understanding, together with suggested activities for the classroom and assembly.

The resource includes worksheets and easy-to-perform scripts and presentations, all with photocopy permission. The twelve themes include caring, fairness, missed opportunities, using our gifts, taking responsibility for ourselves, and treating others as we want to be treated.

ISBN 1 84101 244 0   £11.99
Available from BRF using the order form on page 127 or via the website,
www.barnabasinschools.org.uk

★ ALSO FROM BARNABAS ★

Living Church

Exploring the Christian Church today

MURRAY McBRIDE

For many children, their first encounter with the local church is on a school visit. This book provides everything needed to turn such a visit into a memorable learning experience.

Living Church is a ready-to-use project-based resource. Inside its covers you will find dramatic re-enactments of familiar ceremonies such as baptism and marriage; explorations of physical attributes such as furnishings, architecture, vestments and artefacts; and encounters with the living faith of the local Christian community through the music, colours and storytelling associated with the church.

The project covers 12 key aspects of church life and contains everything you need for a visit to a Christian place of worship with your class or year group, including storyteller's scripts, church construction model, church history timeline, storyboard cards, learning quote cards, activity sheets, project-building ideas and jargon buster.

ISBN 1 84101 399 4   £9.99 (available November 2006)
Available from BRF using the order form on page 127 or via the website,
www.barnabasinschools.org.uk

ORDER FORM

REF	TITLE	PRICE	QTY	TOTAL
394 3	*Through the Year with Timothy Bear*	£6.99		
244 0	*Stories to Teach about God*	£11.99		
399 4	*Living Church*	£9.99		

POSTAGE AND PACKING CHARGES						
order value	UK	Europe	Surface	Air Mail	Postage and packing:	
£7.00 & under	£1.25	£3.00	£3.50	£5.50	Donation:	
£7.01–£30.00	£2.25	£5.50	£6.50	£10.00	**Total enclosed:**	
Over £30.00	free	prices on request				

Name _____ Account Number _____

Address_____

_____ Postcode _____

Telephone Number _____ Email _____

Payment by: ❑ Cheque ❑ Mastercard ❑ Visa ❑ Postal Order ❑ Switch

Card no. ❏❏❏❏ ❏❏❏❏ ❏❏❏❏ ❏❏❏❏

Expires ❏❏ ❏❏   Issue no. of Switch card ❏❏❏

Signature _____ Date _____

All orders must be accompanied by the appropriate payment.

Please send your completed order form to:
BRF, First Floor, Elsfield Hall, 15–17 Elsfield Way, Oxford OX2 8FG
Tel. 01865 319700 / Fax. 01865 319701 Email: enquiries@brf.org.uk

❑ Please send me further information about BRF publications.

Available from your local Christian bookshop.   BRF is a Registered Charity

Resourcing **Storytelling, Seasonal and Drama, RE (including links to PSHE/Citizenship), Circle Time, Collective Worship** and **Assembly**
in primary schools

- Barnabas Live creative arts days
- INSET
- Books and resources
- www.barnabasinschools.org.uk

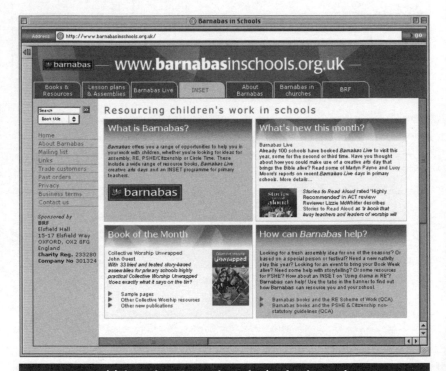

visit barnabas at www.barnabasinschools.org.uk

Barnabas is an imprint of brf

BRF is a Registered Charity